Edition BAES

מה לך פה אלידהו:

Zirl: Edition BAES 2014
www.edition-baes.com

© by Kevin Ring
All rights reserved

Anonymous cover art based on an original photo
by Tom Palumbo www.tompalumbo.com

Layout: Alexander Augustin medien&design, Innsbruck
Herstellung: Books on Demand GmbH, Norderstedt

ISBN: 978-3-9503559-8-7

Kevin Ring

All Day Looking
For His Hat ...

Essays on Jack Kerouac
and other Stories

Edition BAES

Jack Kerouac

born Lowell March 1922. Spoke mostly French for the first few years of his life. Traumatised by the death of his older brother Gerard, something that remained with him for the rest of his life. First novel, *The Town and the City* published in 1950, received few reviews and barely raised any interest. Kerouac met Allen Ginsberg, William Burroughs and subsequently Neal Cassady in the 1940s, these people had a profound influence on his life. Neal Cassady became 'Dean Moriarty' in Kerouac's epic second novel, *On the Road.* It was a book that went through many changes and rejections until published in 1957. The novel brought Kerouac fame, notoriety and ultimate heartbreak and alcoholic breakdown in the ensuing years. A string of works followed, each a reflection of Kerouac's mercurial mind. At the time of his death in 1969 at the age of just forty seven, Kerouac was a lonely neglected figure, at odds with an America at war in Vietnam, out of step with the new culture. The years since have seen a slow restoration of his reputation to the point where his novels are now recognised as doorways to an America that has mostly vanished.

Kevin Ring

born 1951, is the editor of Beat Scene Magazine, a printed paper journal, running since 1988 in Coventry, England.

He has been writing about Jack Kerouac and the Beat Generation since 1972, since he first read *On the Road* and was dazzled by it.

His magazine is dedicated to the work, the history and the cultural influences of the Beat Generation. This has included Kerouac, Burroughs, Allen Ginsberg and Gary Snyder. Also featured have been Richard Brautigan, Charles Bukowski, Lew Welch, Lawrence Ferlinghetti, Michael McClure, Lenny Bruce, Ken Kesey, Jack Hirschman, Gregory Corso, Diane Di Prima and many others.

He also publishes a series of limited edition chapbooks by and about the Beats. Amongst those in the series are Dan Fante, Gary Snyder, Burroughs, Ginsberg, Bukowski, Michael McClure, Kerouac, John Clellon Holmes and Richard Brautigan.

---

www.beatscene.net

Content

All Day Looking For His Hat ...
Kerouac and John Montgomery

Dusting down my box set, *The Jack Kerouac Collection*, issued by Rhino Records way back in 1990, it reminded me that this compact disc three record set has the bonus track *Is There A Beat Generation?* included as an extra track. The original album *Readings by Jack Kerouac on the Beat Generation* was put out by Verve Records in 1958. That album included some absolute crackers from Kerouac, in times when he thought he might still be the next Frank Sinatra, or Dick Haymes. He never gets close in the crooning stakes but his magnificent delivery of writing like *Neal and the Three Stooges, parts one and two*, are arguably Kerouac at his peak. Breathtaking in their verbal gymnastics and tone.

Kerouac had three albums out in his lifetime. *Blues and Haikus*, again on the Verve label and he had two jazzmen whom he fervently admired backing him, Al Cohn and Zoot Sims. Many will have heard these recordings, *The Last Hotel, Book of Blues, Conclusion of the Railroad Earth, Hard Hearted Old Farmer* and *American Haikus*, as they have lately been sent out into the world as stand alone compact disc albums.

The story goes that after the recording sessions Kerouac had hoped that he'd sit listening to what they'd got down on tape, together with Cohn and Sims. However they upped and left, apparently hot footing it to their next sessions. A disconsolate Kerouac was virtually in tears, it is said.

Poetry For the Beat Generation with pianist Steve Allen was the other album in the trio. Again originally issued by Verve, you might recall Allen was the chat show host that accompanied Kerouac when he read the final pages of *On the Road* on national TV. Thirty seven years old, clean shaven, sports jacketed; Kerouac is still in control before his descent into oblivion and alcoholic despair later on. The sound from that TV appearance is captured as a bonus on the compact disc reissue. At three minutes and thirty seconds it is brief but wonderful.

However, it is that *Is There A Beat Generation?* recording that grabs my attention. Not least because Kerouac penned a letter to the forgotten Dharma Bum John McVey Montgomery (Henry Morley), shortly after the fiasco that it was. The event took place at Hunter College Playhouse at Brandeis University on November 6, 1958. Kerouac was heavily drunk, well into the post *On the Road* downturn. The event descended into chaos, despite the presence of English novelist Kingsley Amis, Ashley Montague an anthropologist and James Wechsler, editor of *The New York Post*.

And it seems that a still drunk Kerouac gave an account of sorts to Montgomery in a letter he dived into a day or so later. Jack wrote,

"Dear Monty, old boy I'm going to endeavour to write you a letter tonight tho I am jess about dead drunk after 3 2 3 weeks of bingeing here in my own house where I had to stay and babysit the cats. That James woman was here and helped me keep the place clean. When she read your note saying "Don't let that James woman make a gent out of you," her answer to you is; "Tell him for Jack Kerouac not to make a lady out of me." Many people came here as soon as they learned my maw wasnt here...seamen, girls, dogs, poets, Ginsbergs, painters, neighbors driving over with cocktails in their laps, etc. and the place was a mess of jumping. However, the other night (November 6) I finally made my Brandeis University appearance which I didn't want to do, but they cried and sent telegrams and said I was letting the university down, so I had to go, but I was angry because it was a mess of communists and after reading my prepared article about beat which was very good and funny (Ginsberg said I was "magnificent" which I doubt) I started to call them a bunch of communist shits over the microphone and warning them that if they get what they want, Sovietization of America, they will no longer be able to attend such meetings as we were at. There were boos and cheers."

It would be illuminating to hear the ensuing me-
lee that Kerouac alludes to. Where is it? Locked
in a box in a university store room, just like that
recently discovered first reading of *Howl* at Reed
College in Oregon? He goes onto describe steal-
ing *New York Post* editor James Wechsler's hat
and refusing to give it back, wearing it on his own
head, grabbing microphones and generally being
at the centre of university anarchy. Riots on cam-
pus almost. There is little hint of this later mad-
ness as Kerouac reads. He is in good form, jovi-
al, alert, mischievous. The lively audience laughs
and encourage him; he is obviously a day off from
their more formal lectures. A relief for them. Editor Ann Charters, in her notes surrounding this letter, reports that Jack's reading and the antics that
ensued made their way into a following issue of
the prominent weekly paper *The Village Voice* and
Jack doesn't come out of it well.

Jack's current beau, artist Dody Muller, is in the
audience, Allen Ginsberg also, obviously. Kerouac
tells John Montgomery in the letter that Dody is
the woman for him. He tells him that Dody is related to Wild West outlaws of infamy Frank and
Jesse James, an outrageous lie of course, but Kerouac is having wicked fun in this letter. Yet Kerouac recognised that Montgomery was as outrageous
as he was and possibly realised it would entertain
John. My own long correspondence and meetings
with Montgomery from the 1970s onwards tells

me that John had a particular eccentric wit and loved to mess around with words. He called me 'Nibulungen' for a few years before I worked out what he was on about. Philistine that I am. It was always jazz *and* classical music with John.

Later in this sizeable letter Kerouac encourages John to utilise this wit and write him stuff as if he were just talking to Kerouac, tape record it – Jack encourages. He can see in Montgomery possibilities. John never really made the leap to writer, but he was a prodigious letter writer, sometimes baffling in the extreme. His day job, I think he worked for many years for the US postal service, kept him away from time for writing. Born in Spokane in Washington in 1919, Montgomery had studied extensively and gained a second Masters degree at San Francisco State College in 1964. He was married twice and had a daughter, Laura, with his second wife Dora Rogers. He was the author and editor of a few wild books devoted to Kerouac. *The Kerouac We Knew: Unposed Portraits; Action Shots* was a collection put together by him through his own Fels & Fern Press in 1982. It included nine disparate essays including one from future Kerouac biographer Gerald Nicosia. And a real curio, *Kerouac West Coast: A Bohemian Pilot*. These small but well presented books won't set you back that much.

For those of you still wondering, Montgomery was the guy who went with Kerouac and Gary

Snyder to climb a mountain, it was described in *The Dharma Bums*. The trio begin their ascent but realise they haven't drained their car radiator and knowing full well it will freeze and wreck the car. Montgomery (Henry Morley) offers to go back down and drain it. He does that and catches up with them later. Yet as they embark on the second day's climbing he decides he's tired and leaves them to it and so misses out on climbing the mountain with Kerouac and Snyder. It could be the story of his life.

After Montgomery had fixed their car he returned, Kerouac captured something of his chaotic wit in *The Dharma Bums*, perhaps one of his best loved books, even if it is often overlooked by the know nothing critics, "*In about two hours Morley was within walking distance of us and started right in talking as he negotiated the final boulders, to where we were sitting in the now warm sun on a rock waiting.*

'The Ladies' Aid Society says I should come up and see if you boys would like to have blue ribbons pinned on your shirts, they say there's plenty of pink lemonade left and Lord Mountbatten is getting mighty impatient. You think they'll investigate the source of that recent trouble in the Mid-East, or learn appreciate coffee better. I should think with a couple of literary gentlemen like you two they should learn to mind their manners...' and so on and so on, for no reason at all, yakking in the

happy blue morning sky over rocks with his slaking grin, sweating a little from the long morning's work."

As I look through a bundle of John's letters over the years, Kerouac's description of him, even then as a much younger man, is just so right. He was what you might sometimes call madcap, and Jack obviously tapped into this. I've heard it said a number of times that while Montgomery has but a cameo role in the Kerouac story, Jack drew a wonderfully intuitive and vivid picture of him in *The Dharma Bums*. Montgomery was a witness to the legendary Six Gallery reading where Allen Ginsberg made that breakthrough reading of *Howl*.

I did hear from someone who knew him far better, that onetime John organised a party at his house, when I first had contact with him he lived in a place called Kentfield, and the house was set up, lots of food and drink, people arrived, there was music etc., but no sign of John anywhere. Midway through a great party this figure in full diving gear, goggles, flippers, wet suit and so on, climbed in through a window, waved hello had a drink and sauntered out the front door, John playing one of his madcap japes.

He seemed to know everything that went on; in a letter here he discusses Allen Ginsberg liking the poetry of William Burroughs. Did I miss something? Did Burroughs ever write poetry? I'd like to see those poems.

And John was a patient and thoughtful bloke. He liked the grapevine, the gossip of the Beat circle. Another letter he has typed out some, at that time, completely unheard of Kerouac haikus.

Every cat in Kyoto
can see through the fog

That's one example and just the way John typed them on an old portable in that italic typeface. I can't tell you how good, thrilling even, it was to receive such informative and at times incomprehensible notes from him, now and then it took a week before I could decipher his codelike way of communicating and the penny would finally drop with me.

There aren't many letters from Jack Kerouac to John Montgomery, at least not many that have been published. And certainly no letters from Montgomery to Jack that have surfaced. Surely if Jack kept them they will be in his archive, and Jack tended to retain things and file them carefully as his first biographer Ann Charters has attested to. It would be something to read Montgomery's notes to Jack. They will not be average or dull, that's for certain.

John may not have written much, but he did edit those aforementioned books, and *Kerouac at the Wild Boar & Other Skirmishes* came out in 1986. At the rear is John's jazz poem *Snowmelt from Yesteryears*, which he also published as a neat broadside. There is an essay in that about Jack from his Lowell parish priest, Father Spike Morrissette. Beat Scene sidekick Jim Burns is also featured. Plus a couple of aforementioned titles. In 1988 he published a small collection of his poems, *Hip, Beat, Cool & Antic*. John died on June 5, 1992 at the Kaiser Hospital in San Rafael. He had been hiking and suffered heart problems. There was a neat tribute type book published for him, *John Montgomery: Man of Letters*. And he was certainly a man of letters.

Bill Lawlor, in *Beat Culture: Lifestyles, Icons, and Impact*, says of Montgomery, "*...an indefatigable promoter of Kerouac's work. When Kerouac's reputation was at its lowest, Montgomery's Fels & Fern Press publications and his voluminous correspondence with Beat scholars worldwide helped keep the flame alive....he played an important role in reshaping Kerouac's reputation at the end of the Twentieth century.*"

Whether the *New York Post* editor ever got his hat back from Jack is undocumented.

Jack Kerouac and Sterling Lord
The Long Way Home

Sterling Lord met Jack Kerouac in the Autumn of 1951 when Kerouac brought him his manuscript of *On the Road*. In Lord's book, *Hard Work and Good Luck*, he wrote of Kerouac that, *"...his was a fresh, distinctive voice that should be heard. For more than four years I could not find an editor or a publisher who felt the same way."*

However, Lord had already heard of Kerouac when his friend Robert Giroux, who had edited Kerouac's first published novel in 1950, *The Town and the City*, had called in to see him. Giroux explained that Jack needed a literary agent and he sensed that Lord would be just the man. There was a snag however; Jack was touting his new manuscript as a giant roll of one hundred and twenty feet. It was not a conventional way to present a manuscript.

Lord needn't have worried. He envisaged a problem with a headstrong young author, but Jack had heeded Giroux's well meant advice and by the time he appeared at the basement office of Sterling Lord at East 36th Street, just off Park Avenue, (Though Bill Morgan in his excellent *The Beat Generation in New York* gives the address as 15 E. 48th Street) he had retyped the novel onto standard format paper. The scroll was nowhere to be seen as Kerouac unwrapped his work from newspaper inside his rucksack. It had taken three weeks to retype his work, he told Lord. He also told Lord that Robert Giroux had rejected it.

In his book, lifting the lid off his exceptional and long career as a literary agent, Lord recalls his very first impressions of Jack Kerouac in 1951. By then Jack would have been twenty nine years old. "*Jack was wearing a light-colored weather-resistant jacket with a lightweight checkered shirt underneath. He was handsome, striking-looking and unique in appearance – "diamond in the rough" was the phrase that came to mind. He was courteous, respectful, but we didn't talk at length, and he was leaving the product of years of work in my hands.*"

Of course history tells us that Kerouac had much, much longer to wait before his novel, then called *The Beat Generation*, would find a way onto the best selling lists and place him high in the roll call of Twentieth Century American writers. Indeed it would be six long and frustrating years and Kerouac would write so much more in those years, his golden period in hindsight. The thing that possibly kept him fortified and sane in those six years was the thought that he felt his writing was already 'published in Heaven.'

There were periods in which Kerouac temporarily lost faith with Sterling Lord, with the publishing world in general. It has to be said that while Kerouac was incredibly patient, there is surprisingly little documented about Lord and Kerouac generally. In collections of Kerouac's letters he refrains from writing direct to Lord about progress on marketing his novel until around 1955, Lord has it as June 28 of that year. He said of the incident, "*Jack wrote me that he wanted to pull my manuscripts back and forget publishing. I thought I knew Jack well, so I ignored his request and continued submitting. Twelve days later, he changed his mind and we went on merrily together.*"

It may have been the timely intervention of Allen Ginsberg, the best book promoter and publicist of them all, that swayed Jack into sticking it out with the Sterling Lord agency. On May 27, 1955, Allen had written to Jack from San Francisco. He mailed his letter to Kerouac who was in North Carolina, with his sister and her family. Besides encouraging Jack to send the manuscript of *The Subterraneans* to him so that he could pass it onto Kenneth Rexroth for him to peruse and possibly do something with. At the time Rexroth was an influential figure and especially so at New Directions, a publishing house that might have suited Jack, run and owned by James Laughlin. (*Kerouac enthusiasts will know that New Directions did indeed publish a limited edition of Kerouac's experimental novel Visions of Cody in due course*). But Allen went on in his letter to Jack and strongly advised perseverance. "*As to Lord your agent I guess the best thing is just to leave manuscript with him to work on and let him take his own time, apparently one thing I see, with these people, erratic behavior, or behavior which seems to them erratic, bugs them no end. – Cowley (I hear from Rexroth) was bugged by your pseudonym shot in New Writing.*"

Ginsberg's reference to 'New Writing' was of course Kerouac's publication in *New World Writing*, published by New American Library in April of 1955. In that paperback collection Kerouac, writing under the alias 'Jean Louis', had seen his essay '*Jazz of the Beat Generation*' included. According to Barry Gifford and Lawrence Lee's biography of Kerouac, *Jack's Book*, Arabella Porter at *New World Writing* paid Jack $120 for the piece and went along with Kerouac's insistence on not using his proper name, a tactic Jack used to keep his ex wife Joan Haverty off his tail. It annoyed Malcolm Cowley at Viking. Cowley had hailed 'John Kerouac' in the press and to his New York City circle, for Kerouac to then hide behind an alias was problematic.

It was his first time in print since *The Town and the City*. And Kerouac, while he initially ignored Ginsberg's words of advice, relented and carried on hoping for publication with Sterling Lord. Maybe Allen Ginsberg saved the day with his letter and changed the course of literary history? We do know that Jack replied to Allen on June 1, 1955 from North Carolina and, at that point, was intent on going to New York and speaking to Sterling Lord, he says so in the letter to Allen. But the growing desperation is there in that letter, asking Ginsberg to send him $25 and outlining ideas for Hollywood film versions of his work – for example *Beat Generation* with actor Dick Davalos as Dean Moriarty and Montgomery Clift as Sal Paradise. He also talks tongue in cheek of a non existent production of *Burroughs on Earth*. Maybe he is cracking up? In fact Kerouac had bemoaned his fate and the slowness of progress of his work at Sterling Lord in a May 20 letter to Ginsberg, and pointing out he could have seen his novel published in 1953 had he not refused to publish *On the Road* with Malcolm Cowley. Kerouac goes on at length in that letter how he could have been so much further along with his work and thinks Cowley sees him as an 'unpublished martyr.' Between Keith Jennison, Giroux, Malcolm Cowley and Sterling Lord, Kerouac had plenty of support in New York City's publishing world, but it was translating his visions into something tangible that was just out of reach at that point.

What puzzled Sterling Lord was that two young, highly regarded editors were rejecting Kerouac's manuscript. They were roughly Kerouac's age but failed to see the full merits of his work. They recognised his potential, spoke of his '*enormous tal-*

ent,' yet saw his novel as '*not well made.*' It seemed that while they admired his... '*vigorous prose, his capacity to create a living sense of America,*' they were concerned about the nature of the people he wrote about, they wondered whether these characters would appeal to the mainstream American book reading public. It was 'thanks but no thanks.' Lord was disappointed and so was Jack Kerouac. I wouldn't be the first to mention the new tide of revolution, if you like, that was sweeping across America and the advent of people like Elvis Presley (*Jailhouse Rock* released in 1956), creating a new landscape. Something that Kerouac may have profited from at the time?

Four long years into trying to sell '*The Beat Generation*' as Jack had titled it, the book morphed into *On the Road* and his luck changed. Sterling Lord negotiated the sale of an excerpt from it to *The Paris Review*. The section Kerouac called *The Mexican Girl* appeared in issue number 11 in the Winter of 1955 and then another to the aforementioned *New World Writing* (*Jazz of the Beat Generation*). Those two appearances in print seemed to ignite things just a little. (According to latter-day Kerouac biographer Paul Maher Jr, Kerouac received $108 for this article after all deductions). Did Kerouac's June threat to take his work away from the Sterling Lord agency trigger some hustling on Lord's part? Certainly Gerald Nicosia's biography of Kerouac, *Memory Babe*, hints at a rising desperation in Kerouac at that point. Nicosia points to Robert Giroux's insistence that he didn't want to see any of Jack's spontaneous writings and had rejected looking at Kerouac's *Buddha Tells Us*. (Gerald Nicosia, in *Memory Babe* – does point out that Sterling Lord attempted to sell *Buddha Tells Us* to Harvard University Press who declined the offer). At that point, Giroux, Malcolm Cowley and Sterling Lord were not amongst Kerouac's favourites. Though strangely, in a June 1955 letter to Allen Ginsberg, Kerouac had reported that Robert Giroux had told him he thought *Doctor Sax* was magnificent, but that he didn't want to publish it. Indeed, at that moment in time Kerouac was totally disenchanted with publishers and editors and his sister Nin was intending to handle his publishing affairs. In a May 27 letter to Ginsberg from Rocky Mount, North Carolina, Kerouac wrote, *"Lissen I wrote a full length Buddhist Handbook called Buddha Tells Us and here these rats in New York like, Lord says, "Is it any good?" when I spend my last two dollars long-distancing him, and then Giroux, who'd earlier asked to see my Buddhist works (NOT the others, he was careful to emphasize to Lord) now lets it be known via Lord that he's changed his mind. Meanwhile the manuscript has been sitting neatly typed and ready and idle for a whole month."*

You can hear the indignation, the sense of being out of the loop, away from the big city in rural North Carolina, sleeping and typing on the screened porch at his sister's house, his whole life's work seemingly gathering dust in an apparently uncaring big time agent's office in New York, in Kerouac's mind at least. His fevered imagination must have been working overtime. He was from a small town, his mother, father, sister; they were all small town people, very probably wary of 'city slickers.' It is at this point that Kerouac might have disappeared off the radar, had he carried out his threat to withdraw all his work from Sterling Lord. We may never have heard of him again. The threat was real as Kerouac further outlines in that May 27, 1955 letter to Ginsberg, "*My sister who is taking over my business or the business management of my scripts is disgusted and says we ought to pull the manuscripts off from Lord who hasn't done anything....*"

Now little is known of Kerouac's sister Nin's character, and least of all her business acumen and her experience in the publishing world. She may very well have been a publishing genius given a chance. But it was not to be as Kerouac relented and the situation changed. Not before time. Gifford and Lee relate that Nin and her husband Paul Blake were concerned by Jack's drinking in North Carolina and his continuing preoccupation with Buddhism. It was a puzzle to them. That puzzlement may have sparked Nin's involvement in Jack's affairs; she was worried about her brother. Oh to have been a fly on the wall in the Rocky Mount house as Kerouac discussed his literary stallings with his family back in 1955. Certainly Nin's proposed role as Jack's literary agent seems to have pushed things along.

It was also a fact that Bob Burford, a Denver friend of Kerouac's, they first met in 1947, had interceded on Kerouac's behalf at Sterling Lord's office. As the editor of the influential magazine *New Story*, Burford had a little clout and stressed to Lord that things should really be moving a whole lot quicker. He advocated taking Jack's manuscript to the publisher Knopf and to search for a French publisher for *The Town and the City* (Burford was based in France at the time). Sterling Lord, possibly feeling besieged, offered to try and find a French publisher for *The Subterraneans*. Gerald Nicosia relates that Sterling Lord asked Bob Burford not to interfere. Like Kerouac's sister, Burford was alarmed by Kerouac's drinking and wanted to improve the situation for him.

As Kerouac began to appear in prestigious magazines, Sterling Lord took a phone call from an editor at Viking Press, Keith Jennison. Now Jennison, Malcolm Cowley and Tom Guinzberg at Viking were all fervent advocates of Kerouac's work. The three decided to march ahead with Kerouac's novel and made an offer of $900 against royalties, Lord turned it down flat. Jennison came back with a $1,000 offer which Lord accepted on Jack's behalf. The figures might not seem especially earth shattering nowadays but to Jack Kerouac, fast getting into his mid thirties and keen to avoid being a one novel wonder, it was like manna from heaven. Though Sterling Lord says, *"Jack took the news in stride; it was as if he knew it would eventually be published. and that it was happening now was merely a confirmation of his belief."*

Lord went on to say that Helen Taylor was appointed as Kerouac's editor on the book and she navigated him through many of the technicalities and legal difficulties his manuscript posed, often centering around names that Kerouac had in his book. Lord felt she did a good job, though he did add that it was the last time a manuscript of Kerouac's was ever edited. Lord had later stopped publication of *The Subterraneans* because the editor had hacked at it so much; he called the editing 'totally insensitive.' Kerouac made a firm request that his work not be tampered with from then on. Subsequently Sterling Lord inserted a clause in each Jack Kerouac book contract stipulating *"The publisher may not change a word of the manuscript nor alter the punctuation."*

Whether this worked in Jack Kerouac's favour is open to debate. We all know *On the Road* was his absolute pinnacle in terms of commercial success and whilst books such as *The Dharma Bums*, *The Subterraneans* and others won him many plaudits, his trajectory after 1957 was a downward one. Did his insistence on no interference from editors spoil his chances of success with later works? The recent release of the 'Scroll Edition' of *On the Road* is a pointer. Apparently this is a totally free and spontaneous version, yet many observers have remarked how they expected much more edited material to be revealed. There is less chopped out than many critics expected. My own preference is for the original edited version of *On the Road*.

The build up to the publication of *On the Road* was palpable in Sterling Lord's mind. In an era where television was still in its infancy and newspapers and radio were of paramount importance in the media, (I'm not even sure there were *Mad Men* around then) – interest built in the soon to be published book. July and August of 1957 Lord recalls well, "*I began to feel the growing wave of enthusiasm for it....all the talk was about the Kerouac novel....it was the book they were all excited about.*"

September 1957 eventually came around and by that time Jack Kerouac was in Florida. Sterling Lord has nothing but praise for the man who played such a fleeting yet pivotal role in Jack Kerouac's life, Gilbert Millstein, the writer who penned the superlative laden review of *On the Road* for The *New York Times*. It effectively launched the book into the stratosphere.

With the book finally published Lord phoned Jack in Florida and asked him to come to New York to help promote it. As ever Jack was woefully short of money. Lord left a message for Jack and Kerouac phoned him back asking for a loan of $25 for the travel fare. Jack, unbeknown to Sterling Lord at that time, also asked his then girlfriend Joyce Johnson, then in New York City, to loan him $30. Was this an illustration of Jack's sometimes reported parsimony? Regardless, Jack got to New York City in time to be with Joyce and to walk down to the newsstand on the street and solemnly read the review.

Viking Press head publicity person was Pat Mc-Manus and they took Jack in hand, but things began to go awry pretty soon into the proceedings. Jack didn't show up for events and Lord went to Joyce Johnson's apartment at 65 W. 65th Street where he discovered Jack lying on the floor apparently overcome with a kind of stage fright. It seems he couldn't cope with all the attention. Lord states, *"The shock of Jack's sudden fame caused all sorts of problems for him. I felt he was basically shy, and any time he came to New York City, he had to fortify himself with drink. Initially I tried to help Jack battle his drinking problem, including taking him to a doctor who thought he could help. The doctor turned out to be totally ineffective.*

But I began to realise that, fond as I was of him, I was his literary agent, not his life agent."

It was twelve years after *On the Road* was published that Kerouac died. In the main they were forlorn years, a steady decline in his working life, his personal life, his infrequent appearances in the media were always less than satisfactory, desultory trips abroad in search of his ancestry, rapidly dwindling booksales, almost non existent contact with his old friends, a constant moving of his home, the East Coast, Florida, he became the forgotten man prone to outrageous and conflicting statements. Yet his contact with Sterling Lord, at least in letters, remained. Throughout the late 1950s and through to his tragic but predictable death in 1969 there was an exchange of letters. In some ways this business arrangement was a puzzle, Kerouac had lambasted the whole New York City publishing scene as a conspiracy more than once in letters to friends, yet he steadfastly maintained the link with the man in the big bad city.

In the immediate aftermath of his success with *On the Road*, Kerouac wrote to Lord on January 28th, 1958 and told him he had earned $4,055 minus Lord's 10% fee, during the preceding year. And discussed the making of a record with Steve Allen, he wanted an advance of $500 to do that. It seemed amicable and businesslike. It would be fascinating to read Sterling Lord's letters to Jack. There are no more published letters to Sterling Lord during 1958 but Kerouac appears to be contacting Tom Guinzberg direct at Viking Press (bypassing Sterling Lord?) and speaking with passion about his vision and outlines for his new novel, *The Dharma Bums*.

The thread with Sterling Lord was picked up again on January 8th, 1959. Jack, seemingly in a new mood of optimism and yet a little frustration, wrote to Sterling agreeing to Italian book deals. European sales were going well for Kerouac, Lord having negotiated translations in Germany, France, Denmark, Sweden, Holland, Spain and other places. Significantly he had won a $7,500 advance from Avon Books for *Maggie Cassidy*. In all the hullabaloo over *On the Road* it must not be forgotten that Kerouac had been prolific in his writing with a string of works stockpiled at Lord's office, all looking to be published. In this same letter Jack told Lord that Gary Snyder wanted to work with Sterling with his first book of poems, which was currently in the hands of publisher Don Allen. It all seemed to be working well, though Jack was disappointed that film adaptations of his books seemed slow in materialising. Easy to reflect now in hindsight, but *On the Road* had only been out four months. Gerald Nicosia reflects on this in his *Memory Babe* biography, "*The biggest deal cooking was the sale of movie rights to On the Road. Warner Brothers had already offered $110,000, but getting word that Paramount and Marlon Brando were also interested, Lord decided to hold out for $150,000.*"

Kerouac was rubbing his hands at the thought of some financial security after years of ducking and diving. If Nicosia is right and Lord declined the Warner Brothers offer it was a wrong choice and one could see it as a major turning point in the affairs of Jack Kerouac. Did Kerouac encourage Lord to hold out for more? There is documentation pointing to Kerouac contacting Brando and getting no reply, of course that letter has subsequently been made public.

In her book *Kerouac: A Biography*, (she penned the first biography of Kerouac – Charles Jarvis published one simultaneously –) Ann Charters also illustrates the possibilities open to Jack about the chances of his novel being adapted for the screen. She records that on June 30th Billboard magazine had reported that MGM started filming it, with Marlon Brando as Neal and Theodore Bikel as Jack. The film would feature the music of Earl 'Father' Hines. It was to be the first of so many movie false dawns for the book.

That January letter to Sterling Lord is the only published letter between them to have emerged thus far in 1959. Late in the year Jack was dealing direct with Barney Rosset of Grove Press, who had published *Doctor Sax*, one assumes that Sterling Lord had negotiated that deal? In a May 8th, 1959 letter to Rosset, from Jack's then home in Gilbert Street, Northport – there is a wonderful cameo snapshot of Kerouac's life at that point where he relates how he was on his way to see Rosset at the Grove Press offices when he met a girl and got drunk with her and how *'a thousand people all want to get drunk with him all at once,*' how he is getting old – he is all of thirty seven years old – mentions of Don Allen on the West Coast, typos in future books, fretting about the absence of substantial meaningful reviews in any of the newspapers and magazines for *Doctor Sax*, but his calm confidence that it is a book that will stand the test of time. Life seems a blur for Jack, but you wonder if Sterling Lord is being marginalised as Jack seeks to capitalise on his first flush of commercial success?

A little aside here and a pointer to the close, if sometimes sorely tested relationship between Jack Kerouac and Sterling Lord – in a 1959 interview (much overlooked I might say) Jack did with Al Aronowitz – Jack talked about his house in Northport, saying how it had been described in the media as a '$30,000 mansion.' Jack stressed to Aronowitz that it cost him a mere $14,000 and that he and Sterling had colluded to keep any mention of Jack's house in Northport out of the news. As Jack said, "*I do not want carloads of zen beatnik hipsters scouting my yard and house. How'd you expect me to get work done here? Have you no idea of the number of people who would like to 'meet' me and visit me? Don't you know it runs in the thousands and thousands, mostly teenagers full of insane desire to be big Dean Moriarty's.*"

The infrequent letters to Sterling Lord continued into 1960. Of course Jack used the telephone and it is certain that much went on between him and Sterling through that medium. But they are lost forever. The next documented contact between them was another early January letter from Jack. In that he outlined his plan to secure benzedrine through Four Seasons Press man Don Allen. Jack felt that he would work better under the influence of that drug. More to the point, Kerouac was returning a signed contract for a UK paperback edition of *The Subterraneans* to be issued by Panther. That book eventually appeared in January 1962. Kerouac returned to the subject of Don Allen and expressed the hope that his friendship and business relationship wouldn't get in the way of the working partnership with Lord.

It wasn't until May 1961 that the pair had contact through the mail again. This time Jack was writing from his new home in Orlando, Florida. This was pre-Disney Orlando, a place not too visible on the map in those days. Jack enthusiastically outlined his plans to Lord, future books, going to Mexico, hoping that Lord would visit them in their new air-conditioned home (it hadn't yet become a nightmare), prospects of tennis matches with opponents for Lord lined up. Jack seemed positive and glad to be away from the 'gangsters' of NYC. And he told Sterling he'd received the cheques. Always a good day. Not so good was later in the year when in October Jack again wrote to Lord complaining of his ideas being stolen. The television series *Route 66* had appeared, a feeble and blatant rip off of Jack's 'Road' theme. Other 'Beat exploitation' books had also appeared and they all twisted Jack's principles of what the 'Beat Generation' really entailed. But the good news for Sterling, for Jack, was the completion – on teletype roll – of *Big Sur*. Borne out of frenzied dedication under the impact of massive doses of 'Mexican' benzedrine Jack had carved out the story of his breakdown in California, suffering the catastrophic consequences of alcoholism and a burnt out way of life. Jack told Sterling how proud he was of this work, but now wanted to write something lighter. *Big Sur* had drained him.

By March 31st in 1962 Jack was again talking business and royalty cheques and whether foreign translations in the pipeline with Hungary and other places were just 'baloney.' Jack was happy to leave everything in Sterling's capable hands. Jack apologised for not seeing Lord in New York one last time, defending himself with the excuse he felt ill and needed to get back to the warmth of the Florida sun and mowing his lawn. That's funny; imagine Jack Kerouac mowing his lawn, what a wonderful image. He was so very just like us after all! On the same day Jack wrote a substantial letter to Robert Giroux and explaining how Sterling had procured Jack some 'sedative' tablets which really helped. In fact Lord had brought the tablets personally to Jack's sick bed in New York. That simple act of kindness speaks volumes about the kind of working relationship that existed between Kerouac and Lord.

In mid summer Jack was returning signed contracts for *Book of Dreams* to Sterling Lord and protesting that he couldn't write much for *Holiday* magazine until he had his passport sorted out and he travelled to Cornwall in England, where he figured he had ancestors to look up there. And besides, *Holiday* had tampered with his prose and he wasn't best pleased about that.

Northport was now Kerouac's new home by May 1963 when his next published letter to Sterling appeared. Jack was hesitant about writing an article about 'the Beat Generation' for *Playboy* magazine. He stressed that he could only write it from his own perspective and wouldn't do '*an abstract intellectual discussion*' – that was not his thing. Conversations between him and Lord largely seem to involve magazine articles at this time, perhaps a concern for Kerouac. Though foreign translation royalties got him out of absolute poverty periodically.

Another year passes before Jack's next published letter to Sterling. September 1964, and by now Jack and his mother have relocated from America's East Coast down to the heat of Saint Petersburg in Florida. The move, inevitably, has cost Kerouac financially. One wonders just who was behind the incessant house moves he and his mother made in these years? Jack talks to Sterling about Catalan translations of his writing, the $2,000 Lord found to help finance Jack's move to Florida and other business matters. Jack throws in his love to Cindy. Sterling Lord's wife. It is all cosy. However, tragedy lies just around the corner when his sister Nin, then parted from her husband Paul Blake, dies of a heart attack. It rankles Kerouac, till his own death in 1969, that it is reported in some places that Nin committed suicide, which is a bit of a leap! For a lapsed Catholic that was a 'mortal sin' in Kerouac's eyes. Something not to be countenanced. Years later the record is put straight with a published official account of her death.

As November 1964 rolls around Jack is sufficiently recovered in spirits to convey to Lord that he can't find it in him to write 5,000 words about the late J.F. Kennedy, the assassinated USA President. *"I'm afraid there'd be no point in my trying that, I don't know anything about it. All I have is a brief dream of a few nights ago I couldn't possibly stretch into 5,000 words. Being an irrational dream it might look silly among the other stories."*

As of late, the talk between them is of magazine articles, very rarely novels. Once again Jack sends his love to Cindy, Lord's wife, as she is expecting a baby.

1965 brings a flurry of letters from Kerouac to Lord. In late March Jack is mulling over what to do with original typed manuscripts and notebooks and the possibility of them going into libraries. Of course Jack isn't letting these papers slip through his hands for free, he is in a 'show me the money' frame of mind. As consequent letters to Lord reveal, his weekly income from his books sales globally appears to him to be about $65 a week. Adding to Jack's woes, in an unpublished letter to Lord in late March of 1965 Jack spells out his injuries after he was attacked viciously in a bar, "*Now I have a punctured lung and two broken ribs from a meaningless barroom attack (sneak) on my person. Luckily I got out alive by wrestling the maniac over on his back and then walking out. I broke my own ribs with the off-balance twisting effort. Lung is ok, says the doctor, and ribs are joining and mending. I was alone in a strange bar. I'm through with going out alone and through with hard liquor forever. That's enough of the rough stuff. There was no provocation for these sudden punches into my face. I was just telling my name. Fellow was fast and about 21 and a drifter from the North. (I was stunned and never hit back.) (Again.)*

So I'm home, ribs strapped, no Paris trip. I hope I have some luck from "Desolation Angels" to make up for all the bad luck this past six months."

Jack, full of good intentions, tells Sterling about his new keep fit regime, pushups and the like, for a couple of months he (allegedly) doesn't drink. *Desolation Angels* appears around this time. Jack is delighted with the book. Of course in later years it proves to be one of his reader's favourite books. Reviews are mixed but Jack is heartened that he is getting reviewed in prominent places. One reviewer, Dan Wakefield, seems to have altered his views on Kerouac and gives a generally positive review of the book in *The Atlantic Monthly*. Jack also speaks to Sterling of signing paperback rights to *Desolation Angels* quickly. It is encouraging for him as he recuperates from his injuries suffered in the bar assault. (It seems no charges were ever brought against Kerouac's assailant. Somewhere over the years some fellow has probably related the story of how he decked 'the King of the Beats.' Nobody ever came forward to boast about it, or apologise.)

May 8, 1965 brought a letter from Jack thanking Lord for royalty cheques against *Visions of Gerard*, which had been published by Farrar and Strauss back in 1963. The figure Jack mentioned was a sum of $17.93, even allowing for the times, it was a pathetically small figure. What was bugging Kerouac in this note was the fact he felt his books weren't being distributed. He couldn't see them in Florida anyplace. He complained that Salinger's *Catcher in the Rye* was everywhere, but no paperback editions of *On the Road* or *Desolation Angels*, or any of his titles for that matter. He was mystified. What could Sterling do about it he asked? But the real villains here were Viking who had not anticipated the demand for *On the Road* and couldn't get copies into stores around the country quickly enough. Their slackness back in the late 1950s cost Kerouac and the book had slipped out of the best selling lists quicker than it might have. Nevertheless, Jack was planning a trip to France and asked Lord to send monies owed to him there when he arrived.

Curiously Jack's mother Gabrielle also wrote a friendly letter to Sterling that same day; presumably both letters were dispatched in the same envelope. In her letter 'Memere' repeated Jack's theory that his books couldn't be bought in Florida and that his many friends down there couldn't read his work, she described the situation as 'heartbreaking.' She went on to lament the New York critics who vilified Kerouac without ever meeting him. It was a heartfelt, caring letter. Memere fighting Jack's corner. She concluded the letter amicably by calling Sterling 'honey.'

Financial matters were the tone of an April, 1966 letter to Lord from Jack. In a brief missive Jack thanked Sterling for royalty payments of $7, $22, $17 and $19. Not having other prominent author royalty statements to compare it is difficult to put perspective on these sums. From here they look like paltry figures – no wonder Kerouac also asked Lord about royalty news from England and the second installment of the fee for his Coward

McCann deal, due about then. This presumably for *Desolation Angels*.

He was really feeling the pinch by October of 1966. By then his mother had suffered a pretty big stroke and he was adjusting his life to take care of her at home. There had been what is generally felt by observers – a fiasco of a trip to Europe. It was meant as partly a promotional tour but it rapidly descended into a drinking trip for Jack. Photographs show him asleep on sofas in Italian television studios. Jack wrote to Lord giving him the lowdown on what had happened in Europe and the state of play regarding his home life, "*...my mother is just about going to be permanently paralyzed on the left side.....For God's sake try to find me some assignments, or sell a book to the movies or something. It isn't as tho I were an unknown novice in American literature and nothing could be done. Yugoslavia makes the 17th language I'm translated in.*

I had to ask Mr. Deutsch for help in London, to find a room and to find a quick plane back. He did everything swiftly and sympathetically. Michael Sissons started the ball rolling. But none of us mentioned publishing matters (as you instructed me). In Italy I hardly got a word in edgewise on TV and in question and answer university seminars everybody had long prepared statements explaining me even to myself."

Kerouac carried on to talk about singing in nightclubs, going to the Vatican, losing his luggage at the airport, painting with Franco Angeli, fun in Naples. But he came home to his desperately sick mother, bills and precious little money coming in. He was at a low ebb and while it was amicable and he tagged himself '*your friendly neighborhood gumba*' to Lord, he was letting him know how things were. But what is a 'gumba?'

A month later Jack had arranged to be married to Stella Sampas. In a move designed to suit everyone, they would relocate from Hyannis to Lowell, with Stella taking an active role in caring for Jack's invalided mother. Kerouac was more upbeat in writing to Lord (November 16, 1966) and thanked him for a royalty cheque for *The Subterraneans*, a paperback edition issued by Zebra Press. Jack discusses the artwork on the cover; he's not overly impressed by it and insists that photographs and not artwork should always be used for his covers. Jack always maintained an interest in how his books were designed; journals preserved illustrate his sketches for book layouts. Now Jack was definitely no artist but his ideas had some merit. However his views were never taken seriously. He recalls discussing the proposed artwork for *The Dharma Bums* with Keith Jennison and maintains that a simple photo of him and Gary Snyder sitting under a tree would have done the trick. I've never seen a photo of Jack and Gary together, so that might have been a difficult one to arrange? What is pre-occupying Jack's mind is *Vanity of Duluoz* and he spells out to Sterling his terms.

As Jack entered the final phase of his life he found himself living in Lowell, in the Highlands area of the town, it was a better part of town and the house seemed just right for him, Stella and his mother. However, Jack was going stir crazy with two women and in two early 1967 letters, where he was pretty voluble with Lord; he mentioned his mother's wish to return to Florida. Whether that was just Jack's wanderlust kicking in and using his mother as a cover, who knows for sure? The second letter demonstrates just how meticulous Jack was with his files. He lists all the cash owed to him from largely overseas royalties on his books. They tot up to $3,760 and in addition there is an undisclosed figure pertaining to the German translation of *On the Road*, which surely must have amounted to a tidy sum. Jack wondered when these monies might be coming his way? His family, his constant moving and his alcoholic way of life was costing him dearly.

By March, in a brief crestfallen note, (March 26th) Jack was apologising to Sterling for a drunken, rambling phone call he'd made to him from a bar. Jack hoped it wouldn't spoil their long friendship. He blamed it all on being drunk and the pressure of writing 18,000 words of *Vanity of Duluoz*, which was receiving favourable comments from those who'd seen early drafts. By June Jack was thanking Lord for a loan ($900 I understand) that got him through a difficult period financially. Royalties were coming in very slowly and didn't amount to a lot. Jack said he was able to purchase some groceries and he also cleared the *Paris Review* interview for publication – Ted Berrigan and Aram Saroyan had visited his house and after initial objections from Stella Kerouac they were allowed in. Jack especially warmed to Aram Saroyan and was honoured to be in the company of the son of one of his literary heroes William Saroyan. And he told Sterling this. He was buoyed by editor Ellis Amburn and Lord seeming to like *Vanity of Duluoz*. At this point Jack needed all the boosting he could get. Jack rounded off the year shovelling snow from round his house in Lowell and telling Sterling about that and staying trim and being ever hopeful of *Vanity of Duluoz* turning his fortune around. It was Jack's last letter of 1967, written on New Year's Eve.

In late February 1968 Jack was chasing extra money for additional interview questions pertaining to the *Paris Review* visit of Ted Berrigan and Aram Saroyan. From the tone of Jack's letter his life was a little 'hand to mouth' financially speaking, as he writes Sterling that 'the money came in the nick of time.'

Kerouac's sense of humour never left him. By April 20th, 1968 he was again writing to Sterling in what looks suspiciously like a mock cockney voice and outlining his plans to move from Lowell – a place he now regularly calls 'Stinktown on the Merrimack.' It is in direct contrast to how he had often described the town in the past, a place he professed to love. He was keen to get away. "*But, as I told you on the phone, the people around Lowell here, cheapskates all, as befits Stinktown on the Merrimack, want to buy my house for $25,000, thus depositing me on the sidewalk with paralyzed mother, new wife, and 2 cats, $6,000 short of Equity. The equity I put into this house is close to $10,000, at the drop of an 'onest 'at. The hequity, that is. I'm sticking to my original price. Soon the house will be overrun with snoopers and people who love to look into my bedroom and see me asleep in mid-afternoon naps and say "There he is." (There 'e is.).*"

Jack outlined his further writing plans to Sterling, talking of *Visions of Cody, Beat Spotlight* and *The Second Coming*. And the income this might raise for him. Jack was pushing for an advance. But reviews of *Vanity of Duluoz*, after a buzz pre-publication, had drifted away into a disappointing squib. Kerouac was no longer a 'roman candle,' at least in the eyes of a fickle media and public. His finances were in such a mess that he was on the verge of selling his letters to close compatriots Ginsberg and Burroughs and these did indeed get sold to University libraries. It was a move that must have hurt him to his core. He did have an initial 'top offer' of just $6,000 for his letters to Allen Ginsberg from the well known Gotham Bookmart bookstore in New York. Which was obviously dismissed as history tells us. In an August 24th, 1968 letter to Lord he spells the letters saga out and also talks of appearing on the William Buckley '*Firing Line*' television show primarily to publicise himself and his books.

His mention of *The Second Coming* is intriguing. It never got completed or published in any form as far as I know, yet the very existence of it in Kerouac's mind and writing agenda is indicative of his reliance on his old lapsed Catholic faith, where the idea of a 'final last day of judgment' when God will return at the end of the world to judge us all, must have been firm in his mind. He outlines his book in a little detail to Sterling.

Three days after Jack's August 24th letter to Sterling, his wife Stella pens an emotionally charged letter to Lord. In it she basically fills Sterling in on their cash predicament; royalties have dried up, Jack's mother, bedridden, wants to get back to the warmth of Florida. She asks how the proposed sale of some of Jack's letters is progressing as Lord is evidently handling this business. Stella comes across as articulate and sensitive. Jack must have really been in a hole healthwise to necessitate her writing. There is reference to a *Boston Globe* interview with Kerouac, where 'offensive remarks' were made. Stella is probably talking about an interview that Jack did with Sterling Lanier, entitled *The New Jack Kerouac*, which appeared on February 11th, 1968. Jack evidently said something out of order about people in New York and possibly about Sterling. It wouldn't have been the first time.

There was nothing wrong with Jack Kerouac's memory. In that August 27, 1968 letter that Stella Kerouac wrote to Sterling Lord, Jack who was unwell, added a postscript '

Jack Kerouac
your friendly
neighborhood
basketball star

(See you Sept. 3rd at 4 PM.)

It was an echo of the much earlier note; Jack was now a basketball player rather than a writer as he edged towards an early grave and another agent. The irony is chilling

There was some re-writing of history on Jack's part when he contacted Sterling once more in September. He describes coming up to New York for the publication of *On the Road* and trying to read the famous Millstein review of his book, a column that essentially launched his career, by foraging in a waste basket to read the paper. Of course

Jack is fictionalising what really happened. The reality was that he strolled down to a NY news-stand and bought the paper with Joyce Johnson and carefully read it together with her. Joyce has written of it in the book *Door Wide Open: Jack Kerouac and Joyce Johnson: A Beat Love Affair in Letters, 1957–1958*, she stated, "*At midnight we went out and got The New York Times and found the extraordinary review of On the Road by Gilbert Millstein that immediately established Jack as the avatar of the Beat Generation and one of the most important American writers since Ernest Hemingway.*"

Jack's September 27th letter to Sterling gives a potted history of his life since that fateful day back in 1957, when he became famous, or notorious. He was going to draw upon that life, episodes with the English actor David Niven and other escapades, to come up with a new book, a novel he was ten-tatively titling *Beat Spotlight* or simply *Spotlight*. In honour, of course, of his father, who ran a lit-tle newspaper of that name in Lowell years before. Rather disappointingly Jack appears to apologise to Lord for his wife writing to him and says she should concentrate on washing dishes. It betrays an aspect about him that was typical of the times.

As Jack moved into the last year of his life he was ever mindful of a middle age fast looming up and his penurious state. It seems Sterling Lord had been negotiating to secure the return of his typed manuscript of *On the Road* from Keith Jennison at Viking Press. It had been locked in a safe at Viking since the mid 1950s and Jack wanted it back. He had a growing awareness that his archives might prove of interest to generations to come, how right he was in that thinking! He saw these kinds of artifacts as a kind of pension fund. He wrote to Keith Jennison, he who championed *On the Road* with those like Malcolm Cowley, back in the mid 1950s, and in no uncertain terms told him he desired that the manuscript be sent to Sterling Lord, he wrote, "*Sterling Lord has been waiting for you to deliver this manuscript for years.*" In the letter Jack stressed that if the manuscript wasn't returned he would be contacting his lawyers. He lamented the absence of a movie version of the book and the idea running around in his head that he was '*blackballed*' by the cultural revolution going on in the 1960s in America. (*The little tv show drama with Jack and Ed Sanders springs to mind here, with Kerouac simultaneously positive about the 1960s rebel culture – 'The Hippies are good kids,' to being cranky with Sanders. Jack just wasn't interested in politics and took a kind of Thoreau approach to all that*). Now we know the whereabouts of the famous 'teletype' scroll of *On the Road*, but where exactly is this typed manuscript, the one that Jack brought to Sterling Lord in their first encounter in the 1950s? New York Library Berg archives?

In a further late 1964/early 1965 sidebar to the Jack Kerouac archive situation. Jack did finally discover the fate of one of his 1948 diaries that he'd written in pencil. He and Sterling were checking through items and Jack had always thought it has been stolen from one of his houses in Northport by a 'drunken teenage bum.' However Paul Maher in his book *Kerouac: The Definitive Biography* writes, "*In a brochure he received from the University of Texas at Austin, Jack saw a photostat of a page from the missing journal. He traced the sale back to Gregory Corso, who had stolen the notebook from Northport in the early 1960s and sold it to The House of Books in New York for $1,000 to support his heroin habit. The store had sold the journal to the university.*" Maher does not say what Jack did or whether he received any compensation for the journal from the university. It was typical of the way Jack's life was panning out. And a particularly mean act by Corso. He seems to have done this a few times to various friends over the years, especially Allen Ginsberg. Yet they all seemed amazingly forgiving.

There was bitterness in Jack about how his life was unfurling as he began the descent into 1969.

In the published collections of Kerouac letters there are five during Kerouac's final few months. An odd letter on March 3rd has Jack telling Sterling Lord a joke, quite a funny one at that. And he rounds off that upbeat sounding missive by asking Lord about his royalties. Like, where are they? In April he is talking about his novel in progress, *Pic*. In August he is speaking of an article proposed for the London based literary magazine *Transatlantic Review*, his *Joan Rawshanks in the Fog*, an exceptional piece of writing based around a Joan Crawford film set in San Francisco. Around this time Sterling Lord also negotiated a $1,500 deal for Jack's article *After Me, the Deluge*; it appeared in The *Chicago Tribune*. It was also syndicated under various titles in other places around America.

Fast forward to October 1969 and in the final week of Jack's life he writes twice to Sterling. October 12th he sends Lord the final version of his novella *Pic* and again implores Lord to chase up royalties. From a distance and decades later you wonder, was Kerouac really so broke or was it some kind of running joke between him and Lord? If we are to believe Jack's letters, he is constantly lacking in funds for basics, rents, mortgages, even the bare necessities of groceries. Certainly Jack protests to everyone he has absolutely no funds for travel. Loans and gifts of money from the Sampas family seem to indicate that Jack was indeed scratching around to survive and that it was no charade.

The final letter published from Jack to Sterling Lord was on October 14. He clears up a dedication to *Pic* and instructs Sterling to present the package to English publisher Andre Deutsch as *Doctor Sax* and *Pic*. As a deal. He wants Lord's opinion on the ending of *Pic*. It is a brief and businesslike note. Kerouac died on October 21st 1969.

The pair had united in the Autumn of 1951. At that time Kerouac was still basking in the warm glow of his first book, *The Town and the City*, being published. Whilst it hadn't set the world alight, it was a promising first published novel and a way forward for Jack it appeared. He was 28 at that point. Everything seemed set fair for a wonderful writer's life and his hopes of gaining recognition as a serious writer. In the years between then and the Autumn of 1957 the pair went on a rollercoaster ride and it is clear Kerouac must have sorely tested the patience of Sterling Lord as he waited impatiently for his books to be published. And, of course, Lord had to contend with a radical and fresh writing approach from Jack, and market that innovative new style. Nowadays Kerouac would have had the internet and all that modern technology can offer to promote his talent. Back then he was reliant on the established routes of the time, the newsprint media and his agent, the NY literary grapevine. Lord was incredibly loyal to Kerouac; he perhaps recognised his unique genius and realised persistence would pay off ultimately. There wouldn't have been anything in it materially for Lord as Jack faced rejection upon rejection. And, ultimately, Kerouac knew how staunch an ally Lord had been throughout those long, turbulent years.

Lord, besides continuing to promote Jack's works in the ensuing years, had one more task to perform for him.

"Almost 12 years after On the Road was published, one night when I was sound asleep in my New York City apartment, the phone rang. It was 4:30 in the morning of October 21, 1969. The call was from Stella, Jack's wife. She was choked up with emotion as she told me that Jack had just died."

Before a few days had passed Lord was on the plane to Lowell for Jack's funeral. He travelled up in the company of noted New York City newspaper columnist Jimmy Breslin, a friend of Norman Mailer. Lord recalled the grieving group of Ginsberg, Corso, Holmes, Edie Parker, the Sampas family. The Autumn sunshine beaming through the Massachusetts trees. And much later he recalled how editor Robert Giroux had insisted he hadn't turned down *On the Road* way back. He said he'd never read it as Jack handed him the famous scroll. It was the scroll format that traditionalist Giroux had objected to. Little did Robert Giroux anticipate then that Kerouac had thrust one of the Twentieth century's most cherished literary artifacts into his hands.

The literary partnership of Sterling Lord and Jack Kerouac was mutually beneficial. Today, The Sterling Lord agency is very much a thriving, state of the art concern. I'm not sure what involvement

Lord has in the day to day affairs of the current operation. The publicity for the agency still proudly notes the role they played in the lives and careers of Jack Kerouac (and Ken Kesey) and it is obviously something they hold onto very dearly. It means a lot to them. Much is made of Jack's other great 'partner on the road' Neal Cassady and it was a brilliant if short lived phase. Sterling Lord put up with a lot over the years with Jack's complaints. Lord was steadfast in securing publication for Jack – in the face of resistance to Jack's new writing style – that of spontaneous prose. That fact alone can't have made Lord's task any easier. Yet together they got there in the end. Others may speculate on Kerouac's ultimate fate with another agent. In it's own quiet, get on with it and businesslike, way the partnership Jack Kerouac had with New York City literary agent Sterling Lord was just as significant as his partnership with Neal Cassady.

Some Notes

Memory Babe: A Critical Biography of Jack Kerouac by Gerald Nicosia – Grove Press – 1983

Jack Kerouac/Allen Ginsberg: The Letters edited by Bill Morgan and David Stanford – Viking – 2010

Jack Kerouac: Selected Letters 1940–1956 edited by Ann Charters – Viking – 1995

Beat Angels edited by Arthur and Kit Knight – Tuvoti – 1982

The Jack Kerouac I Knew by Sterling Lord – Publishers Weekly – 2007

Jack's Book: Jack Kerouac in the Lives & Words of his Friends by Barry Gifford and Lawrence Lee – Hamish Hamilton – 1979

The Beat Generation in New York: A Walking Tour of Jack Kerouac's City by Bill Morgan – City Lights – 1997

Door Wide Open: A Beat Love Affair in Letters, 1957–1958 – Jack Kerouac and Joyce Johnson – Viking – 2000

Kerouac: A Biography – Ann Charters – Straight Arrow Books – 1973

St. Jack an interview with Al Aronowitz in Conversations with Jack Kerouac edited by Kevin J. Hayes – Mississippi University Press – 2005

Kerouac: The Definitive Biography by Paul Maher Jr. – Taylor Trade – 2004

Jack Kerouac's VISIONS OF CODY
A Tangled History

When Jack Kerouac made his well documented and touching appearance on the Steve Allen Plymouth show in Los Angeles on November 16, 1959, most people understood him to be reading from his by then famous and even notorious novel, *On the Road*. In fact Kerouac was reading from a far more daring and innovative book he called *Visions of Cody*. That book and *On the Road* had a tangled relationship, *Visions of Cody* at one point being titled *Visions of Neal* and actually part of earlier versions of *On the Road*.

The book that Kerouac read from on the Allen show, with Allen contributing sympathetic piano in the background, had yet to be published. Only a month later New Directions Press, the publishing house founded by James Laughlin and a publisher noted for publishing more experimental writers, would issue a much truncated version of *Visions of Cody* in a limited edition of just 750 copies. All signed by Kerouac.

At the time New Directions included a separate insert with the book, Jack Kerouac said, "*What's been published is only excerpts. There is a 512 page ms. At Sterling Lord's. I wrote it from Octo-*

ber, 1951, to May, 1952, beginning in Long Island and then in Cassady's attic in San Francisco. I had a bed there. That was the best place I ever wrote in. It rained every day, and I had wine, marijuana, and once in a while his wife would sneak in. I wrote it mostly by hand, some typed on Neal's typewriter. (4 chapters of Visions of Cody were taped.) No candles. The candles were for holy books, like Tristessa and Desolation Angels – but they're all holy books."

With only 750 copies issued, 805 if you count in the overrun of 55 copies which were used for New Directions salesmen's promotional samples, the book has become only naturally, a very rare Kerouac collector's piece. In 1959 the hardcover book, '*cover lettered in purple and red, spine lettered in gold, red-orange end-papers. The decorations for the cover, title page, and text are by the author. Issued with a heavy clear acetate dust wrapper,*' according to the Ann Charters Bibliography issued by Robert Wilson's Phoenix Bookstore in 1967, was available for a mere $7.50. Did that include Kerouac's signature? Surely not, even in 1959.

Kerouac had written to New Directions owner James Laughlin, "*....someday this book will be clutched underarm by young American writers like some kind of bible.*" It hurt Jack that only parts of the book, the safer passages if you like, were going to be published. In a P.S. to a letter to James Laughlin at New Directions, written from his 1418 1/2, Clouser Street, Orlando address, Jack says, *"A lot of people are under the misinformed impression that ON THE ROAD as it was published was the fruit of 4 years of editing...there was an edited manuscript but I threw it away and typed up the book as published from the original spontaneous 300-foot roll, and that's why it has that freshness...I hope you soon get a copy of BLACK MOUNTAIN REVIEW where (the new issue) my theories about prose & pure writing are being published for the first time. I'm very serious about this and am still smart enough as a hobowanderer and general Dharma-bum to ward off money – temptations & keep my literature clean.*

There's nothing interests me more than when a man writes whatever comes into his head, & especially when he speaks & spits forth whatever comes into his head...the rest is hem and haw and we've heard enough of that.

In the name of language I really beseech you to consider the importance of full-length Visions of Neal just about the way it is, with a few commonsense bows to Dame Public."

Now it seems that James Laughlin and his New Directions press were early supporters of Kerouac, they had included a small extract in an anthology of theirs, *New Editions 2*, in 1957. The section issued there was *Neal and the Three Stooges*. It was a paperback and just one thousand copies were published. It sold for $1 only. How many have survived and where are they? Do you have a copy? *Neal and the Three Stooges* amply demonstrates the experimental nature of *Visions of Cody*, it is wild, humming with life, idiosyncratic, daring, it sings. Now *On the Road* sang and initially Allen Ginsberg and others in Kerouac's gang thought it was unique but unpublishable in the early 1950s. How they imagined *Neal and the Three Stooges* would be received is fun to think about?

Of course, today we have Kerouac reading this extract; it was included in the boxed set of Kerouac recordings issued by Rhino Records in 1990, as a bonus track to the album *Jack Kerouac, Steve Allen, Poetry for the Beat Generation*. That LP issued in 1959 by Hanover Records. Incidentally, Gilbert Millstein wrote the sleeve notes, following on from his celebratory review of *On the Road* for the *New York Times* two years earlier. And, of course Millstein's laudatory *On the Road* review was a critical element in Kerouac's success. Right place, right time.

Just to sidetrack a little here. Back in 1981 I attended the first official Lowell Celebrates Jack Kerouac event. I'd been visiting Lowell since the early 1970s, sometimes encountering Kerouac enthusiasts who lived in the town, but it was sporadic and Kerouac wasn't talked of much in his hometown.

Often the response was 'Jack who?' 1981 changed all that. For one evening only he was given a celebration in an empty storefront on Merrimack Street, one of Lowell's main downtown thoroughfares. In a gathering of maybe a hundred people at most they played *Neal and the Three Stooges* from a tape recording of Kerouac reading. It was wonderful. I'm guessing that only a few people had ever heard Kerouac read his story before. There were probably quite a few people there who had never heard Kerouac full stop at that time. To coin a phrase, you could have heard a pin drop. Kerouac builds and builds, recreating the world of the Three Stooges, characters so distinctly American, they never really made the leap across to Europe, so they are as American as apple pie. Why Jack himself struggles to recall the name of one of them, he good naturedly fumbles, searching his memory banks to draw his name up, Larry! Yeah Larry, that's it. Curly, Moe and *Larry*! Can you hear him too?

Now I said you could hear a pin drop, but what you could also hear was the quiet sobbing of his wife Stella, who was just a couple of seats away from me. Everyone could hear and it was a moving moment and we all felt for her, being reminded of her husband in such a poignant way, and in public. There were most likely a few other moist eyes in the audience, for Stella but also because Kerouac delivers a brilliant blending of the madcap bopping antics of the Stooges and the frenetic nature and personality of Neal Cassady. He turns back the clock so vividly; he was always inclined that way wasn't he? But the recording, the writing, have to be amongst some of the best things Kerouac ever did.

In England the publication of *Visions of Cody*, in a full version, was delayed and delayed until 1973 and of course Kerouac suffered the disappointment of seeing a favoured work of his go unpublished in his own lifetime. How that must have nagged at him in those desperate years as his star dimmed and he fell into oblivion in the 1960s. Once again Andre Deutsch issued the book with an introduction, *The Great Rememberer*, by Allen Ginsberg. Incidentally Ginsberg's introduction first saw print when it was published in The *Saturday Review*, in December 1972. Ann Charters has recorded that this hardcover edition sold for £2.95, in an age where paperbacks went for about fifty pence a throw.

The sleeve notes for this English edition said, "*This major novel by the late Jack Kerouac, written 1951–52, is one of his most important works. Never before published in its entirety, it has become, over the years, an underground legend. Here is the America of the late forties and early fifties that Kerouac knew so well and celebrated so magnificently – the irresistible lure of the cross-country highways feverishly traveled by Jack Duluoz, the narrator of this book, and Cody Pomeray....*"

The publisher sets the scene so well and you wonder why the book was held over and thwarted? Kerouac's agent Sterling Lord had marketed the book, yet he found only magazine editors willing to take a chance on Kerouac's experimental work. Aside from the aforementioned New Directions appearance, extracts surfaced in *Playboy* magazine during December 1959, for which Jack was paid $1,000. Ten years later Sterling Lord was still finding magazines keen to include excerpts, with the English journal *Transatlantic Review* including sections in 1969 and 1970, these must have been the journals I picked up in Birmingham used bookstores in the 1970s whilst a student there. A book *The New Writing In The USA* was issued by Penguin in 1967 and that too included segments from *Visions of Cody*. Editors were obviously keen to have something by Kerouac in their journals but publishers were afraid of taking on the full work.

What was it that so scared publishers in America and Europe so much? Malcolm Cowley, a pivotal figure in Kerouac's early published career, admitted in the 1970s he didn't rate the book, "*Visions of Cody, in the shape I saw it then, I didn't much like.*" It was most likely the unorthodox approach of Kerouac with his book. Unusual inclusions. Well, for a start, Kerouac and Cassady were into taping themselves and discovering the depths of their conversations as they listened again to where those talks took them. Kerouac had moved in with Neal and Carolyn Cassady on December 27, 1951 and was living in their attic at 29 Russell Street in the Russian Hill district of San Francisco. Often both stoned on marijuana or whatever, their talks threw up some rollercoaster rides. There are roughly one hundred and twenty pages of tape transcriptions in Cody. Jack and Neal allowing themselves to let go, Jack prompting Neal to remember the details, how high the grass was, exactly how high – and fine details about bars at intersections, everything about that bar. They prodded; they cajoled and provoked each other, all the time the tape silently running. Now other writers might have used this recording, these recordings, there were a number of them, for research purposes. Not Jack Kerouac, he felt, at this point, that he was so close to getting to the essence of Neal, of Cody, that they should stand just as they were. Tom Clark in *Jack Kerouac: A Biography* says, "*Sketching was at first strictly an on-the-spot technique, but it quickly developed into a rapid notational method for transcribing from memory and imagination as well. Kerouac's experimental work during the final months of 1951 is documented in the early pages of Visions of Cody.*

The best and purest evidence of the original sketching impulse are the New York and Long Island sketches of October and November. These were scribbled by Kerouac in exhausting ten and fifteen-minute bursts. Each was a dense, detailed "solo" of attention ("Blow as deep as you want to blow," he reminded himself). Sitting in a cafeteria, for instance, he tried to capture the situation at all levels – from the Dutch still-life particulars of surface optics (light reflecting off shiny glass, metal and glazed food inside cafeteria cases, to the psychological, existential nuances of behavior, the loneliness exhibited by people eating in public."

At that time Jack was carrying around with him the Marcel Proust book *The Remembrance of Things Past*. It was such a significant book for him, a cornerstone of his way of thinking, of approaching life and the documenting of it. Record it before it disappears. Many observers have stressed today how Kerouac is important now because he observed and documented things that were disappearing off the map, a vanishing America. Tom Clark is certain that the Proust book pushed Kerouac in the direction of what became *Visions of Cody*.

His friend Allen Ginsberg is unwavering in his admiration for Kerouac and his methodologies. Where others had serious misgivings at including an actual tape transcript as part of a novel, Ginsberg rejoices in it. In his *The Great Rememberer* essay introduction to 'Cody' he eulogises, *"Thus the tape may be read not as hung-up which it sometimes is to the stranger, but as a spontaneous Ritual performed once and never repeated, in full consciousness that every yawn & syllable uttered would be eternal...the tape coheres together with serious solemn discussion of their lives."*

Now they are at home, not on the road, not frantic, Cassady maybe edging towards domesticity, or so maybe Kerouac imagined, he wanted to document Neal, rediscover him, fill in the gaps, the Denver Pool hall episodes, the telegraph pole humming wire football games in the summer dust, before he envisioned Neal slipping into family life, kids, a wife, or wives even, catching the movies of the mind before they vanish. And of course they had the best 'Tea,' to aid their recollections and help their voyage.

The tape recordings were the result of a few nights of talk between Kerouac and Cassady. According to Carolyn Cassady, when speaking to Gifford and Lee in the 1970s, *"Like the Visions of Cody tapes attest they sat night after night and wanted to tell each other stories of their past and every other story they could think of, to get all the details of each other's lives and all their theories about everything. I don't think Jack had any idea at the time that he was going to use them verbatim. I think it was more a friendship thing of getting together, getting it all told, all understood."*

His great friend John Clellon Holmes was another who was allowed to see early drafts of *Visions of Neal*, or *Cody*, whatever Jack was calling it that month. Holmes had recognized a kindred spirit in Jack from the moment they met in the 1940s. He knew they were opposites in personality but both sharing a passion for documenting life around them.

Talking to Barry Gifford and Lawrence Lee for their biography *Jack's Book*, Holmes says of this period, *"He wrote seven, maybe ten other beginnings to the book, and they all didn't seem right to him. This went on for eighteen months at least.*

This was about 1949. Then he became more and more and more hung up by his inability to write the damn thing. He couldn't find the entry into it. And he wrote that whole thing which is in Visions of Cody. Neal's youth, he wrote that on pot."

Gifford and Lee commenting on a long interview with Holmes and his revealing thoughts on the painstaking progress of both *On the Road* and *Visions of Cody* said, *"It reached back to 1946 and 1947, to his first meetings with Neal Cassady and to their first long rides together through "the American night."*

Gifford and Lee also spoke at length about how Kerouac created almost 'ancient epics' based around Neal Cassady and the group of friends around him in Denver in the late 1940s. Jim Holmes became 'Tom Watson' a poolhall hustler of some local repute. While Kerouac was intently making notes in his Denver sojourn of 1948 he felt a hint of friction between them, Holmes was Neal's good friend and Jack was a kind of East Coast interloper, breaking in on their scene.

As the early months of 1952 passed by, Jack began to realize, or believe to an extent, that his 'Neal' book was – at that point still part of *On the Road*, taking on a life of its own and becoming a separate entity. He was waiting on Carl Solomon at Ace Books to make his mind up about whether they were going to publish *On the Road*. Solomon couldn't make his mind up to save his life. It was procrastination that would undoubtedly haunt him for the rest of his days. The book he let slip away. And Kerouac was impatient. Ace had sent him a $250 advance for the proposed book, *On the Road*. Kerouac sent all the money to his mother, says Tom Clark, and continued to live and write in the Cassady attic, all the while sending copies of his latest pages to Allen Ginsberg, his unofficial literary agent. Allen felt the work Jack was producing was wonderful yet problematic, almost commercially unpublishable. Too erotic in places for America in the early 1950s.

With Kerouac it was all or nothing. For his later biographers this period would prove confusing and full of myths and half truths. It was during his time together with Neal and Carolyn Cassady that the three way love affair came into being. Neal, who had turned 26 in February 1952, would be away on railroad work for a few weeks at a time and it does seem that he actively encouraged Jack Kerouac and Carolyn to become lovers in his absence. Kerouac and Carolyn were reluctant, hesitant about this, initially it appears, but with Neal pushing them into it almost, they caved into temptation and it was to prove a good period for all three of them. Jack, buoyed by Carolyn's affection and the security of a warm home environment, ploughed on with his writing, *Visions of Cody* and *On the Road*. By early April 1952 Kerouac had completed what he now called, *Visions of Cody*. Tom Clark reports that, *"His last spasm of effort, concluded in early April, 1952, was a capsule account of all his major travels with Neal – "four trips in 40 states," compressed into 160 typed pages."*

Kerouac immediately dispatched it to Carl Solomon at Ace Books. Jack wanted it to be called *On the Road*. Further, he wanted Ace to issue it in both hardback and softcover. You might ask, why not *Visions of Cody*? It hints strongly at the inability of Kerouac at this point to fully realize he had TWO books on his hands. Predictably Carl Solomon was negative about the manuscript. Kerouac also sent a copy of the same manuscript to publishers Harcourt. They declined. He did get very positive feedback from William Burroughs, who was in Mexico City. In letters to Kerouac and Ginsberg, Burroughs extolled the developments in Kerouac as a writer. It was music to Kerouac's ears. He needed something. The honeymoon three way love affair with Carolyn had floundered. It seems they had gotten too close ultimately for Neal's liking and Jack's stay with them ended in acrimony as Neal and Carolyn dropped him off at the border into Mexico early in May 1952.

In a little aside here, the manner in which that triangle disintegrated obviously hurt Kerouac (and no doubt Neal and Carolyn), in a letter to Carolyn fully eight years later, April 20th, 1960, he expressed some of his feelings about the time he spent with them and in the process writing *Visions of Cody*, "*As for my books, they were published exactly as they were written years ago (CODY mostly in your attic on Russian Hill) so the only thing we'uns can say, you me and Neal, is that they were published...You can remember, tho, from reading Cody, how much I loved that guy and his home and you and the kids – The only thing I regret is the time we fought over money in San Jose and you drove me to Al Sublette's where we spent that money anyway on wine.*"

A word about James Laughlin and New Directions. Kerouac's contact with New Directions regarding *Visions of Cody* seems to have begun around November 1956. An internal letter from one of the staff editors there to owner James Laughlin, dated December 10th, 1956 says, "*The Kerouac manuscript came in Friday afternoon all right, but it was too late to get hold of Sterling Lord, at least by the time I had read it. Otherwise you would have heard from me earlier.*

I did talk with him today, and he talked to Kerouac and called me when Kerouac was in his office. The regular ND terms were agreeable...."

New Directions were to publish both *A Billowy Trip in the World* and *Neal and the Three Stooges* in two of their anthologies during 1957. But the journey for their partial publication of *Cody* in a limited and quite expensive edition was to be full of twists and turns judging by the file of letters going back and forth between Kerouac and James Laughlin between 1956 and 1960. In 1961 when Kerouac was ever hopeful of Laughlin publishing a full version of his book, he was told that censorship issues around Henry Miller had created a publishing landscape that was dangerous and he wasn't prepared to be taken to court for obscenity. And it wasn't just *Visions of Cody* that Kerouac was hoping New Directions would take on. By March 1957, contacting New Directions from Tangiers, Jack spoke up for *The Subterraneans*, *Visions of Gerard* and *Desolation Angels*. He wanted James Laughlin, or Jay as he began to address him, to publish them all. He was mad at Barney Rosset's Grove Press for trying to make 40% cuts in his *The Subterraneans* manuscript. Of course history tells us that Grove and Kerouac came to an agreement and published that book in 1958. Thinking about it now it seems something of a puzzle why New Directions didn't snap it up. But at that point, March 1957, *On the Road* was yet to appear and Kerouac was just another hopeful unknown. Jack wrote in that letter from Tangiers, "*I will no more have my prose cut up than would Paul Bowles or Hemingway or any other conscientious artist...*"

To insert an upbeat note in a story that has so many setbacks and stalled hopes, when Kerouac finally did receive published copies of *Visions of Cody* from New Directions, he was ecstatic. Writing to Laughlin from his Earl Avenue home in Northport, Kerouac wrote, "*Dear Jay, I just looked at VISIONS OF CODY and I thought of writing to you: "You Dog! You realized that my prose was like an endless poem and you snuck it in Miltoneseque verse lines to make the poets know!" And I almost cried.*"

He continued to suggest that they get together, as they had both threatened to do for a few years. Jack was happy. It wasn't the full unabridged work, but it was something.

In May 1961 an upbeat Kerouac sent a hearty letter to his agent Sterling Lord. In this letter Kerouac proposed a plan of action over his 'Duluoz' legend. He wanted Lord to negotiate deals for full publication of *Visions of Cody*, alongside books he was calling *Visions of Julien*, *Vanity of Duluoz* and Memory *Babe*, those three still to be written. A healthier Kerouac, or so he insists, was up for the fray and wanted to get going.

The middle and later 1960s were a slow decline for Kerouac, it is well documented. Some commentators have tried to dress the period up a little, denying that they were in any way miserable forlorn years. That Kerouac had friends in Florida and Northport and so on. Certainly there will have been fleeting moments for him, but the overall drift was a downward spiral of all engulfing gloom. Nothing really happened, as far as we know, regarding *Visions of Cody*. What became of *Visions of Julien* and *Memory Babe* is anybody's guess. If you have a secret access to the safe containing any remaining Kerouac manuscripts, please tell us.

By June 1965 Jack was again trying to wrestle Sterling Lord into doing something with *Visions of Cody*. In a letter specifically addressing all the potential of that as yet unfulfilled manuscript Kerouac wrote from St. Petersburg in Florida, "*We take "Visions of Cody" and mark out page 95, top of it, "Tape Recording of Cody Speaking" and go to page 108, bottom of it, "report you well and truly" – and submit that as an excerpt for publication to Playboy for no less than $2,000.*

This is because so many people on my trip told me they wanted to see "Visions of Cody" but couldn't find copies of its limited edition anywhere, and would at least like to see a piece of it.

At the same time, as an example of tape-recording transcription, it's of other than literary interest to all the technicians and characters who read Playboy."

Jack was naturally trying vainly to push James Laughlin into a full version of *Cody*. As his career dipped it was again significant that Kerouac was unable to get Lord to convince either New Directions or *Playboy* to take up his offer. In a sad and final postscript to the Kerouac and New Directions connection, James Laughlin – after a lull in correspondence that stretched to a few years – wrote to Jack in June 1968 to remind him that the contract they had over *Visions of Cody* was terminated and that his letter was official confirmation of that. Laughlin was warm, friendly, courteous as ever and told Jack it was a wonderful book and deserved to be in print. But lamented the fact that publishing it fully was beyond New Directions. He reminded Jack to renew the copyright on the book in 1988. Little did he know. The book was stalled.

Back in January 18th, 1955, Jack had penned a substantial letter to Allen Ginsberg. Kerouac is increasingly disillusioned with everything; his books seem to come up against a brick wall of publishing indifference. Obviously his mind is fixed on those manuscripts that are gathering dust with his agent Sterling Lord, Jack reminds Allen of some of his favourite parts of 'Visions of Neal,' "*One of the best parts in Visions of Neal is that part about Saturday Night Red Neons Making Me Think of Chocolate Candy Boxes in Drugstores, remember? – good for Crazy Lights –* "

It must have frustrated him no end to see his hard work so unloved. Shortly after Jack briefly fell out with agent Sterling Lord and asked that he send all his unloved manuscripts back. Shortly after Jack's *Jazz of the Beat Generation* appeared in the paperback volume *New World Writing*, at that point Kerouac changed his mind and asked Sterling to forget what he'd said.

Jack contacted Sterling Lord again in July, 1955, asking about *Joan Rawshanks in the Fog*, amongst a lot of other material. The article is a particular favourite of mine. Capturing the film actress Joan Crawford filming on an especially foggy evening in the streets of San Francisco, some of Kerouac's most atmospheric writing. The name of the movie was *Sudden Fear*. Biographer Dennis McNally, in the treasure of a biography – *Desolate Angel: Jack Kerouac, the Beat Generation, and America* – said the movie bombed. But he went as far as to say that the essay was arguably the best thing Jack ever wrote. He further described it as the 'New Journalism' fifteen years early. Yet Kerouac would have a long wait for this essay to appear.

Three sections from *Visions of Cody* eventually appeared in *The Beats* edited by Seymour Krim in 1960. (Krim was a helpful guy for Kerouac). This was a USA paperback anthology that ran to 185,000 copies no less. It was issued by Fawcett Publications. In the UK it finally went into *The Transatlantic Review*, (number 9) – an English paperback literary journal in the Spring of 1962. Tellingly, or confusingly, Ann Charters bills it as a section from *Visions of Neal* in her '*Jack Kerouac: A Bibliography*' published by Robert Wilson's The Phoenix Bookstore in 1975. There were other intermittent sections published in journals during the 1960s.

Today there is wider acceptance of Kerouac's innovative book. Perhaps everyone needed forty years or more to better appreciate the things he was attempting. To catch up with him. He was probably ahead of his time. Matt Theado, in *Understanding Kerouac*, describes the book as 'a masterpiece.' And speaks of Kerouac's search for 'IT.' That elusive factor. And, of course, Kerouac's spiritual quest, for meaning, was so overlooked by shallow critics of his era who drowned his real focus under a sea of exploitation and hip nonsense. Theado likened Kerouac at this 'Cody' point to James Joyce and William Faulkner. Theado reminds us of the date that Kerouac made his great breakthrough stylistically with his notion of 'Sketching,' handed to him by his friend Ed White. October 25, 1951. With this new tool Kerouac made giant leaps with *Visions of Cody*. Writing in the last ten years Matt Theado notes, "*The scenes that Kerouac sketched include the ones that begin Visions of Cody. Thirty brief sketches, most of them barely a page long, describe an old diner, the Caprico B-movie theater, the Third Avenue elevated subway track, and various other scenes. Cody is rarely mentioned. Yet the*

scenes as they appear would not have been record-
ed except for Cody's influence."

American critic John Tytell was equally as ef-
fusive, in a conversation with John Clellon Holmes in 1974, he said, "*Visions of Cody, for me,
is when Kerouac really comes into his own. Dr.
Sax also has that sense of inventive leaping, that
unique power and freedom of form.*"

And Tytell was the guy asking Holmes the questions! Holmes thought, in response, that *Visions
of Cody* was as eloquent as any prose he ever read
in his life. Dennis McNally bracketed Kerouac's
Vision of Cody/Neal alongside jazz great Charlie
Parker and abstract expressionist artist Jackson
Pollock for his innovation and experimentation
alone. McNally later likened the daring of *Visions
of Cody* to the out on a limb comedy routines of
Lenny Bruce and Lord Buckley. Surely Bruce and
Buckley were picking up on Kerouac's flights of
imagination years later?

Dennis McNally's biography is simply superb; remember he was penning it during the 1970s, without much of what we take for granted these days.
The Jack Kerouac archives not as accessible as now,
it was new territory and there were no computers.
McNally's skill in linking Kerouac in with his times
is wonderful. He deftly placed him in amongst the
context of his landscape, the musicians, writers, art-
ists. He saw the crass exploitation that he endured
and overcame to a degree. But that's a digression.

So McGraw Hill finally got around to publishing the book in full in January 1973. It was a substantial hardback. A paperback edition followed in the USA in 1974. Much too late for Kerouac, dead five years. But it must have played a part in the gradual resuscitation of his reputation, which by then was in absolute tatters. Many of his books no longer in print. He was a fallen icon, ignored, derided, forgotten. A drunk fat guy prone to crass outbursts on the odd American TV show. Hopelessly out of sync. Allen Ginsberg writes in his introduction, "*Jack Kerouac didn't write this book for money, he wrote it for love, he gave it away to the world; not even for fame, but as an explanation and prayer to his fellow mortals, and gods – with naked motive, and humble piety search – that's what makes Visions of Cody a work of primitive genius….*"

Perhaps the best way to capture the difficulties Kerouac encountered with *Visions of Cody* is to return to comments made by John Clellon Holmes. Throughout the later 1940s, through the 1950s and into the vortex of the 1960s, Holmes and Kerouac remained big friends. Of course they had their moments, writerly competitiveness surfaced from time to time. You only have to read the letters between them to gauge the heat at points, mostly emanating from a jealous Kerouac, stunned by the initial success of Holmes with novels like *Go*. But the bond was always tight. Talking to Gifford and Lee for *Jack's Book: Jack Kerouac in the Lives & Words of His Friends*, Holmes said, "*When he sent me Visions of Cody, and even Doctor Sax – Doctor Sax came first – I thought, man, no one's going to publish this. It's brilliant. Its youth. It's something absolutely new and unique and important, but no one's going to publish it. I'll never forget that afternoon. It was snowing. I was living on Forty-Eighth Street on the fifth floor of an old tenement, and I read that whole damned book Visions of Cody in one day. And I was depressed, not by the book, but by the fact that I knew he wasn't going to make it with this book. He wasn't going to get through. Nobody but me and Allen and a few people would ever read it, it seemed to me. I thought, "Oh, God, Jack! Why can't you write something that can get published so somebody can understand what you have?" In my foolishness it seemed he was being perverse. I was of two minds. I still am. In those years, in the fifties, it seemed to me most important that somebody come to understand him. They haven't to this day.*"

There are so many instances of breathtaking prose in *Visions of Cody* that it is a task to select just a paragraph or two to illustrate the camera like mind of Kerouac, so intent on mapping everything he sees that others miss. A certain slant of light here, a faded sign, clouds that say something, real characters and all their foibles, the patina of life on everything and everybody, sparks flying here and there, I've chosen this one for the sheer exuberance and joy of it all....

"...*So when the gang gave up the precious table and let their empty Cokes plop in a floorbox with a "So long fellers" and left the hall to jump in the car, a '37 Ford belonging to Evans, for the ride north to Wyoming about eighty miles, the sun just then going down in vast unobserved event above the madding souls of people, and Cody above the objections of everyone else insisted on driving to show his skill, but then really fantastically wheeled the car right clear out of town with beautiful spot-shot neatness and speed, the guys who were pre-pared to criticize his driving and give pointers or stage false hysterical scenes forgot they were in a car and fell to gabbing happily about everything – Suddenly out on East Colfax Boulevard bound for Fort Collins Cody saw a football game go-ing on among kids in a field, stopped the car, said "watch" ran out leaping madly among kids (with noble seriousness there wearing those tragic lumps like the muscles of improvised strongmen in com-edies), got the ball, told one blondhaired boy with helmet tucked underarm to run like hell, clear to the goalpost, which the kid did but Cody said "Further, further," and the kid halfway doubting to get the ball that far edged on back and now he was seventy yards and Cody unleashed a tremen-dous soaring wobbling pass that dropped beyond the kid's most radical estimate, the pass being so*

high and powerful the boy completely lost it in ey-
rieal spaces of heaven and dusk and circled fool-
ishly but screaming with glee…..."

This is just a mere half a page. Wonderful, just wonder full.

Books consulted

Jack's Book: Jack Kerouac in the Lives & Words of his Friends – by Barry Gifford & Lawrence Lee – Hamish Hamilton – 1979

Memory Babe: A Critical Biography of Jack Kerouac – by Gerald Nicosia – Grove Press – 1983

Jack Kerouac: Selected Letters 1957–1969 edited by Ann Charters – Viking – 1999

Jack Kerouac: A Biography – by Tom Clark – Thunder's Mouth Press – 1984

Visions of Cody – by Jack Kerouac – Andre Deutsch – 1973

Understanding Kerouac – by Matt Theado – University of South Carolina Press – 2000

Desolate Angel: Jack Kerouac, the Beat Generation, and America – by Dennis McNally – Random House – 1979

Kerouac and the Beats: A Primary Sourcebook – eds Arthur and Kit Knight – Paragon House – 1988

Joan Rawshanks in the Fog – Jack Kerouac, included in Transatlantic Review No 9, 1962

First Night of the Tapes – Jack Kerouac – Transatlantic Review No 33/24, 1969

NOTES

I wanted to thank the people at New Directions Press, and the Houghton Library at Harvard University Archives, Mary Haegert, Leslie Morris and Heather Cole – for assistance in tracking down letters from Jack Kerouac to New Directions Press and from staff at New Directions also.

A MEMOIR OF KEROUAC
AND THE FIFTIES

Interview with Helen Weaver by Kevin Ring

For a brief interlude, a sometimes turbulent phase, Helen Weaver, one of the two Helens, was Jack Kerouac's girlfriend. She was with him at the point where he signed the book contract for his ground shaking novel *On the Road*. Though by then he was something of a roustabout hard drinker, the pair shared times together. They were to part and reunite, express lasting love for each other in passionate and caring letters. But it was a doomed affair. After years of deliberation, procrastination and hesitation Helen Weaver has finally penned her memories of those times. It is as much a picture of the era as their relationship. It should stand alongside *Minor Characters* by Joyce Johnson. Beat Scene interviewed Helen about her book, *The Awakener: A Memoir of Kerouac and the Fifties.*

Your new book, *The Awakener:* A Memoir of Kerouac and the Fifties, has been a long time in the making?

You could say that! I started the book on Good Friday in 1990. I sent it to the printer on Bastille Day, 2009. (Jack was a French Catholic!) This book has been in the works for nineteen years and it's been in the back of my mind for fifty: ever since that day in November 1956 when Jack and his friends landed on my doorstep and he entered my living room, my bedroom, and my life. Why did I wait so long? I wanted to be a better writer. The Kerouac file sat on my computer for years pending the courage to complete. Perfectionism, fear of hurting people's feelings, fear of failure, fear of success, innumerable false starts, and just plain laziness: all these have exerted the necessary pressure to keep this story from being told. Through it all I never stopped feeling that I had a responsibility to present my little slice of history to the world, that, like Jack, I had a duty to record my experience to the best of my ability.

You talk about the various reasons for delay. Did Liz Von Vogt's book, Edie Parker's – did those books, Joan Haverty is another – did they push you on?

Not really. I would have written my book if no other woman had come forward with a memoir of Kerouac and/or that time. The only one I was really aware of was Joyce Johnson's *Minor Characters*, which I consider a little masterpiece, and the first book about Jack in which one can clearly hear his voice. Although I was inspired by Joyce's book it would be more accurate to say that I was intimidated by it. She, after all, is a novelist, and she had a great deal more material to work with: she stuck by him a lot longer than I did. I suspected that my book would be compared with hers, and that actually slowed me down rather than pushed me on.

You've set your recollections of Jack Kerouac in context with the broader sweep of your book? I can almost feel the brownstones and fire escapes of New York City. Why is the city so vital?

I'm glad you can feel the brownstones and fire escapes! Why is New York City important? With all due respect (you Brits invented the novel, I believe), New York *is* the publishing capital of the world! Where else would an English major with literary aspirations want to live? And where else but Greenwich Village would a rebel like me want to be? Especially one who was, as Roger Straus put it, "*a little dykey around the edges.*" Offbeat people are drawn to cities, and New York is the greatest city in the world. Like I said, it was be there or be square! The city was the magnet for Jack and Allen–both from mill towns that had fallen on evil days (I just learned that Paterson, New Jersey, was in much the same depressed state as Lowell, Massachusetts)–as it was for most of the characters in my book: Helen Elliott from Omaha, Lucien Carr from St. Louis, etc. Gregory Corso was the only native New Yorker of the Beats.

Helen, Jack gave you the name Ruth Heaper in his book. What did you make of that? How did you feel about being in his book?

Well, if you'll recall, the first time I went to bed with Jack he quoted the Bible to me, *The Song of Songs*: "Thy belly is like an heap of wheat set about with lilies," and so on. So that's how he came up with the name Ruth Heaper.

It was fine with me. I was proud of being in *Desolation Angels* and very touched by his portrait of me. He seemed to have forgiven me for telling him to "hit the road, Jack" three years before.

Thinking of the bible, Jack was fascinated by Dwight Goddard's Buddhist Bible; did he talk much about that with you? And has it had a bearing on your life since?

Well, Jack did read me a passage from the Buddhist Bible the morning after the day we met. He was unpacking his rucksack, and he took that book with him everywhere. The particular passage he read me was very beautiful:

"All the mind's arbitrary conceptions of matter, phenomena, and of all conditioning factors and all conceptions and ideas relating thereto are like a dream, a phantasm, a bubble, a shadow, the evanescent dew, the lightning's flash. Every true disciple should thus look upon all phenomena and upon all the activities of the mind, and keep his mind empty and self-less and tranquil."

The language was beautiful, but the ideas didn't make much of an impression on me at the time. Jack was always telling me that nothing was real, it was all a dream, and that was all very poetic, but I didn't really believe it. I was twenty-five, and just beginning to make my peace with the so-called real world. I suspected that his Buddhism was just a big excuse for doing whatever he wanted to do. But years later, I was drawn to Buddhism myself. Like Jack (and unlike Allen), I never made a lasting connection with a Buddhist teacher, and perhaps as a consequence my practice never really took hold. But I still think the Buddhists have the best philosophy, the most accurate understanding of reality, of any organized religion.

And as I got older I decided that Jack was right: life is a dream.

Your journal beginning January 1st 1957, was that inspired by Jack's journals?

I'd never seen Jack's journals. I knew he took notes on anything that struck him in those little pocket-size notebooks of his – he called it "sketching" – but I don't remember his showing me what he had written. I had kept a diary in high school, which helped me get through those difficult years, and I tended to take pen to paper when anything was particularly bothering me. I think I was inspired less by Jack's journals than by the stress of living with him and the pain of loving a man who couldn't give me what I needed. I didn't start writing until things started to go south. Writing as therapy!

You talk of things 'going south.' One incident with Jack – where you have dinner with Jack at Henri Cru's. It seems like a bad night. Could you see it coming?

Not really. I remember being really upset by how unhappy he seemed to be, especially after we had had such a wonderful time when Jack met my parents just a few days before. Jack and I were both nervous about that, and against all the odds, taking him home to Scarsdale was a great success. But at his old friend Henri Cru's, he slipped into a depression: didn't touch his elegant dinner, just guzzled the expensive wine and sat there scat singing to himself and drumming on the table.

I've wondered about his seemingly fatalistic approach to the world, melancholia – 'all life is suffering.' It must have been difficult for you, a young woman looking forward to all that life can offer – with this often brooding (depressed?) man?

Yes. I was twenty-five to his thirty-four, and I had probably never heard of the Buddhist teaching that life is suffering. It certainly didn't appeal to me. I was particularly shocked when Jack said that it was a sin to bring children into the world. That seemed very extreme. I think I thought Jack was saying that life had no value, and that was not true at all. Jack also believed that "life is holy, and every moment is precious." I understand that a more accurate translation of the Buddha's teaching would be "life contains suffering," or "life contains unsatisfactoriness," which I think anyone would agree with.

But I didn't care for what Allen Ginsberg called Jack's "gloomy harping on the First Noble Truth" of the Buddha, that life is suffering. Buddhism provided Jack with a metaphysics that justified his own intuitive sense of impermanence and loss. I wasn't ready for that. I hadn't experienced death yet. But as I aged, and especially after my father died, I came to accept the idea that life is tragic. In the end, I came to agree with Jack.

You were together with Jack when he signed his contract for *On the Road,* I understand? That must have been a moment to savour? Can you recall if it had any big impact on him and you as a couple? It must have lifted the mood surely?

Yes, I was with Jack at the turning point of his life, just before he became famous. You'd think the contract with Viking would have been a cause for celebration, but oddly enough it really wasn't.

Allen told me that Jack was so nervous about seeing his editor Malcolm Cowley that he consumed a pint of bourbon in the elevator. When Jack told me that Cowley had accepted the book and it was finally going to be published I was happy for him, but he didn't seem that happy himself. Any celebrating he did was with the boys: Allen, Peter, Gregory, and Lucien. Jack and I celebrated Christmas together, but not the signing of the contract.

You wrote a letter to Jack after he came home late and drunk with Lucien Carr? Could you elaborate on that?

The night before he signed the contract Jack and Lucien went on the town in a blizzard. They came roaring into our apartment in the middle of the night, drunk as lords, yelling at each other and crashing into the furniture. (My roommate the other Helen was out on a late date.) They put *My Fair Lady* on the record player and started singing along with Stanley Holloway at the top of their lungs on "Just a Little Bit of Luck" and "Get Me to the Church on Time."

Well, I had to get up and go to work the next day, and I lost it completely. I got out of bed and flew into the living room and actually pounded Jack with my fists and tore out a chunk of his hair. Jack always maintained that was the beginning of the end of his looks.

When they finally left they took Helen's dog with them – to Helen's horror when she got in from her date at 5 am. Miraculously, the dog survived. And after that Lucien, who previously thought I was a wimp, revised his opinion and started referring to me admiringly as "Slugger."

The next day I felt terrible, and wrote Jack a letter apologizing for beating on him but basically telling him he had to get his act together, or find someplace else to live.

And I wanted to ask you about the revelation about your close encounter with Lenny Bruce. I never saw that coming?

Neither did I! How many times does your hero, whom you've worshiped from afar, call you on the phone and want to come over? Maybe I cheated by putting my time with Lenny in the book because after all, that was the sixties, and this book is supposed to be about the fifties. But it seemed like part of the same *zeitgeist* of free speech and rebellion, and Dan Wakefield said, put it in!

Would you do things any differently with Jack, with hindsight?

Although I regret my lack of respect for his writing until years after he died, I really can't imagine doing anything differently. I certainly could have been a better friend to him at the end of his life when he was so lonely, but I was who I was, and I accept that. It took me years, and a whole process, to appreciate him as a writer; but that was true for mainstream America too. In a way, I was representative of my time.

You found Jack's Lowell beautiful, where others have described it as horrible. What did you find there?

Those red brick factories are the oldest ones in America! The industrial revolution started in Lowell. Plus, I love those lovely old Victorian houses, and the "humpbacked Merrimack" running through the town. Even the fact that it's almost impossible for visitors to find their way around Lowell adds to its mystery and charm.

It is easy to overlook other aspects of your book; Jack is such a powerful figure. You write about Susan Sontag and your connections as a translator. An important phase of your life?

Working with Susan on the Artaud *Selected Writings* was a delight and an honor, as she was a hero of mine. What a great mind that was, and what a voracious lover of life.

You say you initially read *On the Road* "with the jaundiced eye of the disappointed lover..." Had you been disappointed all those years? That's a lot of heartache to carry around. Did you always feel that way?

Oh, my no – I think I forgave Jack early on. After all, we were only together for a short while, and I had a shocking number of affairs, some of which were far more painful than my time with Jack. Jack was so fundamentally innocent. He was just incapable of a sustained relationship with any woman other than his mother, as he freely admitted himself.

And going to Lowell seems to have been some kind of epiphany for you. Liking the place (as I do – though it's not conventionally pretty) and finally sinking into his books, his read aloud poetry of it?

Yes, going to Lowell in the nineties was the catalyst for finally getting serious about this book. In some strange way, I felt closer to Jack after he died. And he wrote so beautifully about Lowell. His description of the flood of 1936 in *Doctor Sax* is a great moment in American literature.

Helen, another thing I must mention is a section where you are with Dan Wakefield in Greenwich Village and you imagine that YOUR Greenwich Village is still there underneath the modern one. What an image: the Subterraneans really subterranean.

Well, Jack said it best: "Nothing is real, it's all a dream." In the end, the dream is more powerful than the reality. I call Jack "The Awakener," but the irony is that the reality he woke us all up to is the reality (which the Buddhists understand) that all is illusion, that life is a dream.

Finally, what is the significance of the title? Why did you decide to call the book "The Awakener"?

Thought you'd never ask! For at least four reasons.

First, a silly one: because when Jack lived with me, I couldn't get enough sleep.

But on another level, his books–especially *On the Road* – woke up an entire generation, from the long dream of the fifties. And through books like *The Dharma Bums*, Jack played an important role in introducing Buddhism to America. That was a major wake-up call, for the very word Buddha is Sanskrit for "awakened one."

Finally, there's an astrological reason which has to do with the prominence in the charts of the whole Beat generation of the planet Uranus, which rules revolution and art, and is known to astrologers as "the Awakener."

So I guess you could say the title – and maybe the whole book – was written in the stars.

Helen Weaver's *The Awakener: A Memoir of Kerouac and the Fifties* was published by City Lights Press in 2009. ISBN 9780872865051

JACK KEROUAC
THE VOICE IS ALL

Interview with Joyce Johnson by Kevin Ring

Biographies written by people who actually knew their subjects are like gold dust. Therefore Joyce Johnson's *The Voice Is All: The Lonely Victory of Jack Kerouac* is one to be taken note of. Johnson writes from experience, from a time when Jack Kerouac was unknown, a guy with a lot of unpublished manuscripts. After a few years research into her old friend's archives in the New York Public Library and reflecting on events from over fifty years ago, Johnson has arrived with a fresh look at a writer close to her heart – and dare I say it, close to all our hearts. And Johnson has a surprising finish to her biography. I asked her some questions recently during a busy time for her promoting the book.

Can I ask you a first and probably predictable question? When did you first begin to feel the need to write this book?

I have felt the need for a book like this for about three decades – ever since the succession of Kerouac biographies started coming out. With the exception of Tom Clark's biography and *Jack's Book,* the Kerouac various writers portrayed frankly did not bear much resemblance to the man I had known intimately for nearly two years, even though much valuable material had been gathered. But the reliance on interviews really warped the picture, I thought, for a good many of them basically portrayed the public Jack – the persona he assumed under the influence of alcohol. I was fortunate enough to see another side of him – sensitive, tender and very quiet, during the periods when he was sober. Jack did me the great favor of taking my writing seriously and giving the kind of encouragement I could not have gotten from most men. As a fellow novelist, although a beginning one, I understood and accepted how much his writing was at the center of his life and how his immersion in it affected his moods, of course there was a great deal I didn't know – and that Jack had never told me, or maybe anyone. But all of that was locked up for forty years in his inaccessible papers, so the biographers who preceded me were really laboring at a disadvantage.

You should know that I kept begging both Ann Douglas and John Tytell to write about Jack, because each of them had such an excellent and sympathetic understanding of Jack and his place in literature, but neither of them took me up on this idea. In 2007, when I learned qualified scholars could at last have access to the Kerouac archive,

I was seized by the urge to write Jack's biography myself and to center it on the development of his work. My feeling was that with that emphasis my biography could tell quite a different story. I have to say that I also felt this idea was crazy – the last thing I should be embarking upon at the age of 72 with my lame left knee and arthritis in my wrists. I tried to resist temptation for a while, but found myself thinking about what I would put into such a book all the time. My original intention, as you know, was to cover Jack's entire life, but given my focus, I felt by the time I'd written three quarters of the book that I could end it in 1951 and cover all the really essential points, while suggesting Jack's trajectory into the future. I was fortunate to have a wonderful research assistant, Brittney Canty, who was studying writing at the New School; we met at the library three times a week and she developed an excellent sense of what I was looking for and what was important in the vast mass of Kerouac material. Otherwise, I was on my own. I applied for two grants, one at the library, which would have made life much easier, since it was difficult for me to carry my computer back and forth, but did not receive them. I worked my way through Jack's life chronologically, absorbing and reflecting on the material, and steadily writing when my impressions were freshest as well as researching I abandoned myself to the unfolding story as if I were writing a novel and never quite knew what I would discover when I opened the next file. (I learned early as a writer not to operate by a detailed road map but to know one's general direction and leave oneself open to discoveries and insights along the way). Once I found the right voice for the book, which took a couple of months, writing it was a very exhilarating experience, and I miss it still.

Joyce, that ending it so early will really surprise people, but given the events after the mid 1950s – when it seems Jack gradually slipped into decline, not so surprising? Too painful for you to document?
I've read Carolyn Cassady say Tom Clark's biography is a good one too, he understood Jack. What is it, Clark being a poet?
Do you feel unburdened of a weight, something done after a long thought process?
We live in an age when there's a tremendous appetite for hearing all the sordid details of a celebrity's decline. One of the things I've always felt is that with the exhaustive accounts of Jack's tragic last years we were losing track of what he achieved as a writer, which is really the most important thing to focus upon. It's gratifying to me that some of the writers who have responded to the biography felt that I had restored Jack's dignity as a human being and as an artist. Had I continued to cover Jack's life, I would have tried to maintain

that balance, but in the end I saw no need to go over all that old ground, including the ground I covered in *Minor Characters*. Which can now be read as a kind of sequel.

I wanted to tell a different Jack Kerouac story than the ones that had been told before – to make his development as a writer as compelling to read about as the story of Madame Curie discovering opium. Despite my previous plan to deal with Jack's entire life, I realized my narrative was working toward a natural and organic ending when I was writing about the great breakthroughs Jack had in late 1951 – at the same time he realized he was helplessly slipping into alcoholism. As a novelist and memoirist, I have learned to let myself be guided by the unexpected insights that come to me during the process of writing – they surface from a deeper place than the conscious mind. Of course Jack knew this too.

Because I was a firsthand witness to so much that happened from 1957–58, I have always felt an obligation to set the record straight regarding Jack and the Beat movement, since I have been painfully aware of so much distortion and misconception. I tried to do this in *Minor Characters*, then realized gradually over the years how more there was to learn and understand. I now feel and hope this obligation has been discharged

Yes, I think Tom Clark had a particularly good understanding of Jack because he was a poet himself. The other biographers have been academics and journalists, rather than creative writers. My own experiences and discoveries as a writer helped me to understand Jack's. I know that my own psychological well being very much depends upon whether or not I'm writing.

The urge to write a biography of Jack that would focus intensely upon the impact of his Franco-American heritage and upon the process through which he eventually found his voice first came over me in 2007. I had long felt the need for such a book, but the idea of doing a biography at first, especially at my age, was daunting. For one thing, I had never done archival research. For another, I realized such a book would take years to write and that I might have serious health issues before I ever completed. Yet I was intrigued by the idea of writing in a new genre, and the challenge soon felt irresistible. I decided I would write Jack's story chronologically, researching as I went along and being open to whatever I might find – from that process, my narrative would find its form. It is the way I have always worked as a writer, with the exception of my first novel, where I doggedly stuck to a very detailed plan.

Joyce, about your daily writing, on the period writing the book, can you let us into a little of the routine, the NY Library, Brittney helping you, what was that like?
Did the archives surprise you in any way?

For three years, I spent three days a week at the Berg Collection, taking notes on the archival material (no one is allowed to transcribe an entire file from Jack's papers). I was fortunate in finding a wonderfully sensitive assistant, Brittney Canty, a young writer, who had an excellent sense of what I would find especially relevant or important. For about two years, the two us worked side by side at one of the long oak library tables and discussed our findings over sandwiches in Bryant Park over lunch. The other days of the week, I spent writing – sometimes from early morning into the night. Since I was always working from my latest notes, the material and my first impressions of it were fresh in my mind. I found the whole experience tremendously exhilarating.

I found what I had hoped to find in the archives – the evidence of Jack's profound preoccupation with his ethnicity (something he never talked about to friends) and a wealth of material about his development as a writer, for his journals contain a record of that process. I also found much that surprised me. For example, I assumed that when I looked at files from the late Forties, I would find detailed accounts of on-the-road adventures and transcriptions of many of the conversations he'd had with Allen and Neal. Not so. Instead I was struck by how few notes he actually took (there is no record of any of those conversations). He wrote *On the Road* out of memory and imagination. I also found that only a few weeks before Jack wrote *On the Road*, he wrote an autobiographical novella *(La Nuit Est Ma Femme)* in French in one of his notebooks. When I read that, I realized that in the French voice of that narrator, Jack found the voice he would soon give to Sal Paradise. Now I find so much that is French in the prose of *On the Road*. Even the quote from a letter of Jack's, "The Voice Is All," which is now the title of my book is very French I realized only recently. In English, one would say, "The voice is everything," while in French it would be: "La voix, c'est tout!" So you see I continue to learn things about Jack I didn't know.

Three days a week for three years is real dedication. I'm intrigued to read about your research in the archives, does a librarian stand guard while you look at papers? After all these are precious records. The novella *La Nuit Est Ma Femme*, has that ever been published anywhere? Do you think it would be something for the future? Or would Jack be annoyed if it were published?

Yes, the entire Berg Collection, which is behind a locked glass door, is closely guarded. You have to prove you are doing legitimate research in order to be admitted and leave all your personal belongings with the exception of a wallet and a pencil (no pens allowed) or a computer in the downstairs checkroom. The place is freezing because the cool temperature protects the papers that are stored there. The files you request are brought out to you one by one by the very helpful and knowledgeable librarian on duty. I was not allowed to Xerox any of Jack's papers or type a complete transcript of any file. I took notes by hand or on my computer, sitting at a long oak library table on an old leather chair (very unsuited for using a computer). I kept looking wistfully at a small antique desk in the corner and thought I might be more comfortable there. When I asked if I could use it, I was told, "No! That was Charles's Dickens' desk!" The accompanying chair had a cane seat. When the library acquired it in the 1930's, Fiorello LaGuardia, the legendary mayor of New York, who happened to be quite overweight, sat down on it during a ceremony and went right through the caning. I grew to love my days at the library and quite often ran into other Kerouac scholars. The Kerouac archive seemed a bigger draw than the other collections. Now the papers of William Burroughs are there too.

Jack never even typed *La Nuit Est Ma Femme*; it's still in one of his notebooks. It should definitely be carefully translated by someone who can capture Jack's voice and brought out in a dual language edition. It's really an unknown gem.

Can I take you back to page 13 of your book and talk to you about Jack's apparent shame at being

alive, due to the Catholicism that surrounded him and his brother's death. Do you think that really stayed with his into his adult life? That and his Franco-American heritage seem to have been twin edged swords for him?

And on page 49 you talk of him saying 'pay me the penny after.' From his comic book days in Destouches – giving you something of his past – it is like he waited all those years to do that for somebody and he did it for you. How wonderful is that?

I do think Jack may have suffered from lifelong shame and guilt that had its roots in the death of Gerard. His mother unwittingly contributed to Jack's suffering by emphasizing that Gerard, about whom Jack had ambivalent feelings, was a saint and that he had died so that Jack might live. She clung to this legend of Gerard for her own comfort, but what an almost unthinkably heavy burden to place upon a child!

Jack's Franco American heritage was a source of both pride and shame for him. The stereotypical view of Franco Americans during the period when Jack was growing up was that they were a backward and primitive people. It was unusual for someone with Jack's background to move away from his community into the American mainstream. Once he left Lowell for New York, he found no else like him, no one who spoke his intimate language, and his journals indicate that throughout his life he was conscious of being an outsider in America – that even among his friends, he didn't really fit in. He had grown up conscious that he didn't speak English like a true American, and perhaps for that reason formed the habit of remaining silent in his classes – as well as in social situations later on in life , where he was shy and very quiet unless he had been drinking. Whenever he was hurt or troubled, he retreated into the Franco American side of his personality. This was especially true in the 1960's, when he secluded himself in the "little Canada" he shared with his mother. Ironically, the feeling of not being "American" enough seems to be part of the American character, since we are a nation of immigrants.

Yes, the discovery of the origin of "Pay Me the Penny After" was a great moment for me, since the phrase had always seemed so strange and I didn't understand why Jack had suggested it as a title for my novel. It did have a relationship, however, to his original title suggestion: "Fly Now, Pay Later," the slogan on a TWA ad we saw in the subway the night I met him in 1957.

Brave of you to mention the puzzling aspect of Jack and his mixed feelings about Jewish people. I seem to recall Jack, near the end of his life on that forlorn trip to Europe with members of his wife's family, crying with remorse when he realised the extent of the Jewish suffering in Europe. I can't recall, did he visit Dachau or Belsen?

It bothers me that he could harbour such unkind views, this man who wrote so beautifully and seemed such a tender soul.

And you talk of William Saroyan, who is sort of neglected these days, unfashionable even. Yet he was such an influence. And they met didn't they? As Jack encountered Aram Saroyan much later while being interviewed for the Paris Review?

Jack's anti-Semitism had to be addressed. It was a prejudice he had grown up with; both his parents had a real hatred for Jews. We also forget these days how widespread anti-Semitism was in America, as well as throughout Europe, in the prewar period – we find it even in the work of the best writers of the period. For Jack, who had so many Jewish friends, the hatred seemed to be an abstraction that came and went along with his moods and the contradictions in his nature. He was definitely embarrassed by his father's virulent prejudice. I was surprised when I read *Desolation Angels* and saw that the first word he used to describe me was "Jewess" – suggesting that I had a certain otherness for him. But during our relationship, I had never had any indication that my Jewishness was an issue for him. Probably the reason that he never proposed marrying me, though once he seemed close to doing so, was that he could never have brought a Jewish bride home to his mother.

Did Jack actually meet William Saroyan? I know he met Saroyan's son.

You refer to quite a number of unfinished and unpublished works, 'I Wish I Were You,' & 'I Bid You Love Me.' What are your feelings about this type of work being published posthumously? I'm thinking of 'Hippos' and 'Orpheus' and so on.

I think it is very helpful for Kerouac scholars to have early books like *Hippos, Orpheus*, and *The Sea Is My Brother* available in print, because otherwise they would have to go to the Berg collection to read them. But I don't think they really help Kerouac's literary reputation, since the average person reads them and finds them weak with little or no knowledge of their place in Kerouac's development. I think we have seen the same problem with the release of texts Hemingway did not seek to publish in his lifetime. One exception here is *Atop an Underwood*, which was put together so well by Paul Marion, in which we can see the young Jack teaching himself to write, trying out different things, and sometimes producing exceptional passages that remind us so much of his later work. On the other hand, I kept coming upon gems in the Kerouac archive that really should be gathered together and published so that everyone can read them, because they represent Jack at his best. I know I would find more if I continued my research past 1951, which I am very tempted to do if I could get the go-ahead to put together such a collection. One of these gems is of course the very important "*La Nuit Est Ma Femme*," which

French Canadian scholars like Gabriel Anctil have been excited about for years. That should be an elegant, separate book with superb accompanying English translation that captures Jack's voice.

....

With her diligent and sustained research into the Kerouac archives at the New York Public library and the knowledge that only came with direct, first hand contact and experience of living with Jack Kerouac and being with him and his friends, this biography has a depth and understanding that surpasses all those biographies that came before. Nothing can trump being there and this ace card is the key factor in Joyce Johnson's outstanding biography. She has the awareness to step back and analyse, not in a full blown academic way, but as a keen observer might, reflecting on insights gained over fifty years ago. This awareness is coupled with a strong desire to reveal truths about Kerouac's working methods. Johnson discovers, I suspect much to her surprise, little or no evidence that Jack kept notebooks on his first trip West to see Neal Cassady and the rest of the Denver gang, Ed White, Hal Chase and others. For sure he took his famous spiral bound notebooks with him, but they weren't used very much. *"Jack would return to Ozone Park in the fall of 1947 with remark-*

ably little down on paper in the form of notes on his recent adventures. Carolyn Cassady would later swear that she had seen him standing on Denver street corners jotting down everything he saw and heard – a "fact" that immediately made its way into Kerouac biography. But the truth is that apart from a paragraph listing the names of places he passed through, Jack recorded very little of what he saw and experienced during the course of his first trip to the West."

That paragraph of places names must have been the template, the springboard from which Kerouac kicked off from. His memory sparked into life by the towns he passed through. He wasn't called 'Memory Babe' for nothing. And let's be clear, Joyce Johnson isn't debunking Jack or admonishing him, her discovery really points out his magnificent imagination and powers of recall, combined with a surefire way of welding it all together.

Throughout the biography the long days spent with the Kerouac archives, a substantial one and constantly growing it seems, pays off with discoveries and re-evaluations of episodes and characters that colour Jack's life. What happened to the ninety nine paged screenplay that Jack sent to Columbia Pictures at Henri Cru's instigation? It seemed like a serious enough project on Jack's part, hassled as he was by Cru into doing it. And Bea Franco. The Mexican Girl. She's always remained an elusive, ethereal figure in the Kerouac canon. I would imagine that many might have thought she was a fictional creation by Kerouac over the years. Of course she wasn't and while Joyce Johnson spells out that Jack stretched out the period that he actually spent with Bea, it was indeed a real phase of his life, unlike anything else he had ever experienced in his young existence. Joyce Johnson talks of letters between them, half a dozen from Bea, after Jack left the cotton fields of California for the East Coast. Bea was keen to come to see Jack; she had been impressed with him. The letters seem to reveal that given a little encouragement Bea, with her little son, would have travelled East. Jack replied little and his final note to her told her he was planning to join a ship and travel. It all faded away at that point. What happened to Bea Franco? Jack's story 'The Mexican Girl' was a prime factor in his emergence as a famous writer when it was published in *The Paris Review* in 1956. Did Bea Franco get to see herself portrayed in the recent film version of *On the Road*? Where exactly is Bea Franco? She sounded like a beautiful young woman.

The Voice Is All – The Lonely Victory of Jack Kerouac by Joyce Johnson is published by Viking Press, 375 Hudson Street, New York, NY 10014, USA. ISBN 978-0-670-02510-7

Note

Bea Franco of course has been *rediscovered* by Tim Hernandez in his terrific part fact, part fictionalized book *Manana Means Heaven* (University of Arizona Press – 2013). Bea died shortly before this book was published and sadly just before the film *On the Road* came out, where she was portrayed by the actress Alice Braga.

さんは書きました:

さんは書きました: